Rhetoric Online

POLITICAL COMMUNICATION

FRONTIERS IN

Bruce Gronbeck and Mitchell S. McKinney
General Editors

Vol. 22

PETER LANG
New York • Washington, D.C./Baltimore • Bern
Frankfurt • Berlin • Brussels • Vienna • Oxford

Barbara Warnick
& David S. Heineman

Rhetoric Online

The Politics of New Media

SECOND EDITION

PETER LANG
New York • Washington, D.C./Baltimore • Bern
Frankfurt • Berlin • Brussels • Vienna • Oxford

Library of Congress Cataloging-in-Publication Data

Warnick, Barbara.
Rhetoric online: the politics of new media /
Barbara Warnick, David S. Heineman. — 2nd ed.
p. cm. — (Frontiers in political communication; v. 22)
Includes bibliographical references and index.
1. Rhetoric—Political aspects—United States.
2. Internet—Political aspects—United States.
3. Persuasion (Rhetoric) 4. Intertextuality.
I. Heineman, David S. II. Title.
P301.5.P67W37   302.23'10973—dc23   2011033873
ISBN 978-1-4331-1329-1 (paperback)
ISBN 978-1-4539-0194-6 (e-book)
ISSN 1525-9730

Bibliographic information published by **Die Deutsche Nationalbibliothek.**
Die Deutsche Nationalbibliothek lists this publication in the "Deutsche
Nationalbibliografie"; detailed bibliographic data is available
on the Internet at http://dnb.d-nb.de/.

The paper in this book meets the guidelines for permanence and durability
of the Committee on Production Guidelines for Book Longevity
of the Council of Library Resources.

© 2012 Peter Lang Publishing, Inc., New York
29 Broadway, 18th floor, New York, NY 10006
www.peterlang.com

Printed in the United States of America

Contents

Preface

Since the first edition of *Rhetoric Online* appeared in 2007, consumers' uses of Internet-based technologies have become progressively more dispersed and variegated.

In the 2010 midterm elections, for example, 73% of adult Internet users (representing 54% of all U.S. adults) went online to get news or information about the elections (Smith, "the Internet"). Furthermore, The Pew data indicated:

> One quarter of all US adults (24%) got most of their news about the 2010 elections from the Internet, and the proportion of Americans who get most of their midterm election campaign news from the Internet has grown more than three-fold since the 2002 campaign. (Smith, "the Internet")

It is also significant that far more than in the 2006 midterm contests, online users took advantage of a wide variety of affordances, including social media and Twitter, to track developing political events and discuss public issues with others. In 2007, when the first edition of *Rhetoric Online* was published, Facebook had 20 million users and Twitter had approximately 350,000 accounts ("Number of Twitter Users"). Today, they have more than 500 million ("Timeline") and 200 million users, respectively (Shiels). The Pew data indicated that in 2010, "Ten percent of internet users ages 18–29 took part in online discussion groups, compared with 6% of 30–49 year olds and 5% of those ages 50 and up" (Smith, "How Americans").

In light of the ongoing changes in both the capacities and uses of Internet-based public political activity, we feel that it is important to track developments in online politics so as to better understand how the introduction of new media forms and practices has reshaped the functionality and effects of public communication in the early decades of the twenty-first century.

Consequently, this edition of *Rhetoric Online* will consider the nature of the public sphere and the effects of online public discourse on users' responses to political developments generally (chapter 1). Furthermore, we will consider advances in new media technology as well as recent research in mass communication, critical cultural studies, and other fields. In doing this, we expect to provide a means for readers to recognize and understand the roles of online activity in people's understanding of and participation in major political and social issues.

To focus that discussion, we provide an extensive overview of the role of new media in the 2010 midterm elections, highlighting how the political context in the aftermath of a highly charged, highly mediated 2008 campaign contributed to particular uses of new media by candidates, voters, and the news media in 2010 (chapter 2). As part of that discussion, we emphasize the ways in which the interests of rhetorical theory and criticism might be productively applied to new media. It is particularly important to do this in light of substantial developments in the forms, uses, and access to online content that have developed since the first edition of this book was made available in 2007.

While in the early years of the Internet online interactivity was viewed as a relatively "new" concept, in the second decade of the twenty-first century interactivity has become ubiquitous, taking place in personal and major news-related blogs (chapter 3). It has become not only commonplace but essential in enabling proponents and opponents on various issues to refine their thinking through online discussion, deliberation, and mutual agreement. Interactivity has enabled people to develop ideas and become aware of aspects of many issues that are of interest to them in their personal and public lives.

Building on these notions of interactivity, we also consider a specific kind of new media text in an analysis of viral video (chapter 4). In focusing on viral video, we define the term to clarify what differentiates a "viral" video from one that is not, assess the role of memetics for understanding certain kinds of Web-based discourse, and discuss the importance of rhetorical uptake and circulation for analyzing these videos. We do so most extensively through a case study of Lady Gaga's YouTube video "A Message from Lady Gaga to the Senate" concerning Don't Ask Don't Tell legislation.

An interesting dimension of online campaign activity and commentary has also been extended in the form of intertextuality, or cross-reference between social context, public events and developments, and the political scene. Intertextually developed content offers many opportunities for social commentary and public amusement, but it also raises public awareness of the missteps of public figures and their shortcomings through satire and parody (chapter 5). This sort of information serves to increase the public's knowledge of aspects of the political scene about which they might otherwise be unaware. Thus, intertextuality consistently plays a role in peoples' knowledge of and interest in political developments and events.

Because, in the time since the first edition of *Rhetoric Online*, social networking (and social media more broadly) has become central to much of what constitutes online activity, we offer some thoughts about how rhetoricians might examine a variety of political, commercial, private, and public texts that are mediated through these still-emerging technologies (chapter 6). By drawing on several venerable rhetorical concepts, such as Kenneth Burke's theory of identification and consubstantiality and Maurice Charland's constitutive rhetoric, we explore the possible ways in which social media might facilitate in the construction of certain audiences and identities. As part of this discussion, we also consider some of the limits of using traditional methods of rhetorical criticism for the analysis of new media.

While much of the book focuses on institutional and electoral politics and the role of new media therein, we also examine the significance of anti-institutional politics online through a discussion of politically motivated computer hacking, or hacktivism (chapter 7). We suggest that a case study of hacktivism offers insight into the complications facing anti-institutional politics on the Web, especially for critics interested in how protest might function differently in digital contexts. Considered in and against the history of radical protest movements and a context of recent legislation addressing cyber security, we discuss how both hacktivist activity and responses to it might be theorized through Paul Virilio's work on strategic presencing.

Our hope is that this book will provide a useful resource for enabling increased understanding of the roles played by online interactivity in shaping public knowledge and awareness of the forces engendered by debate, discussion, and deliberation in enriching public understanding of major cultural and political issues. The role of the Internet in this process is significant, and continued study of persuasive online communication by rhetorical critics and analysts is vital to its effective development and the public's potential to benefit from its use.

The production of this book would not have been possible without the assistance of many individuals who supported our work. These include the series editors and especially Bruce E. Gronbeck who provided encouragement, criticism, and advice throughout the development of the book, the staff at Peter Lang Publishing, and Peter Kracht, Editorial Director at the University of Pittsburgh Press, who offered advice and assistance early in the project. We would also like to thank student researcher Georgette Elmes, who helped us with some of the research into social networking.

Barbara Warnick would like to acknowledge the contributions of her husband, Michael R. O'Connell, for supporting her work, both intellectually and as "technical advisor." David S. Heineman would like to acknowledge his wife, Brianne Heineman, and his two-year-old son, David James Heineman, for their support and encouragement throughout the writing process.

The Internet and the Public Sphere

During the past twenty years, there has been increased concern among sociologists, political scientists, and communication scholars about the health of the public sphere as a space for democratic deliberation and debate. To some extent, the present angst about the public sphere has its origin in Jürgen Habermas's 1989 book, *The Structural Transformation of the Public Sphere* (originally published in German in 1962). In that work, Habermas presented a genealogy of the bourgeois public sphere in Europe, which he viewed as having its origins in the seventeenth and eighteenth centuries. Using extensive citations from published documents of the time, Habermas traced the rise of the bourgeois public sphere as the result of a combination of factors, including increasing literacy, a rising commercial and trade sector, and formation of a bourgeois class.

He noted the importance of the private sphere within its historical context, viewed as the realm of commodity exchange and social labor imbedded in the conjugal family as it related to salons, the theater, reading practices, and social gatherings of the day. The private sphere served as a resource for the public sphere, a space in which people read, discussed, and wrote about opinions, issues, and ideas in coffee houses and public meeting places. An analogous phenomenon in our current media environment might include the contexts of personal blogs, social networking, and mobile communication as "private spheres," since much of this content is not necessarily intended for public deliberation.[1] Habermas described the characteristics of his construct of the bourgeois public sphere, which included widespread rational-critical debate, equality and association among persons of unequal status, freedom from censorship of free expression, and the opportunity to reach consensus about what was practically necessary in the interest of all persons.

The Public Sphere as a Contested Concept

The Habermasian public sphere has to some extent become an idealized construct against which the venues and practices for public discourse in other eras have been assessed. It had its shortcomings, some of which were described by Nancy Fraser. She noted that the bourgeois public sphere excluded many groups of people, especially the illiterate, women, laborers, and other groups in society (Fraser 60). Its exclusive emphasis on debate and rational-critical discussion also elided other forms of communication, such as performative and aesthetic expression, which unified social groups and enabled identity formation (Warner,"Abbreviated Version").

Because of these objections, the viability of Habermas's version of the public sphere as a model of public deliberation has been widely challenged; thus the very idea of a public sphere is highly contested among scholars. Some critics of the concept, such as Fraser, have noted that the public sphere as conceived by Habermas incorporates "a historically specific and limited form of the public sphere," which Habermas called the "liberal model of the bourgeois public sphere" (Fraser 58).

In contradistinction to an idealized public sphere that would include groups from all sectors and strata of society, promote transparency, and encourage rational critical debate, the Habermasian public sphere was therefore compromised by a number of exclusions, and Fraser has maintained that "declaring a deliberative arena to be a space where extant status distinctions are bracketed and neutralized is not sufficient to make it so" (60).

Other scholars have observed that the idea of a single, unitary public sphere is of limited value. For example, Gerard A. Hauser, in his book *Vernacular Voices*, invoked the idea of a "reticulate" (that is, networked) public sphere, comprised of a plurality of publics, and he described these publics as "*emergences* manifested through vernacular rhetoric" (14). In shifting the focus away from a unitary bourgeois public sphere and toward interactions that constitute the mundane transactions of words and gestures that mark our quotidian encounters in public discourse, Hauser has opened up the possibility that we might want to consider public sphere discourse in terms of a multiplicity of spheres emanating from a variety of perspectives. He described civil society as "a web of discursive arenas in which members of society engage each other in ongoing dialogues that continually confront public problems, constitute publics, and challenge [each other] within and across domains for the formation of public opinion" (49).

Another scholar of public discourse, Michael Schudson, has also questioned the uniqueness of the bourgeois public as an ideal. He expressed reservations about its influence as an unprecedented framework for civic engagement. He wryly noted the fallaciousness of an idea expressed in current critiques of American politics and culture that emphasizes a "decline from some great and golden age" (143). The Habermasian public sphere invoked a sort of nostalgia—a belief that the virtues historically associated with deliberation and public debate have somehow been *lost*. In questioning this assumption, Schudson enumerated features that should characterize a healthy public sphere, such as citizen attendance at town meetings; voter participation in elections; a nonpartisan press; and inclusion of groups from various strata of society. By consulting historical records, however, Schudson found that voting percentages in the late nineteenth and early twentieth centuries fluctuated from 80% in 1844 to a very low point in the 1920s. Furthermore, literacy levels among the general populace in the late eighteenth and early nineteenth centuries were very low. Decisions reached during this period by many governing bodies at the state level were rarely made public, and then, as now, newspapers often boosted the parties they represented. After describing the potentials for bribery and intimidation at the polls during the same time period, Schudson viewed the imagined historical public sphere as a chimera, and he concluded by reminding his readers that "thinking through the conditions and possibilities for more rational and critical, fair and fair-minded, political practices in our own day will not profit from maintaining illusions about the character of the public sphere in days gone by" (161).

Public Discourse as Circulation and Response

In surveying work conceptualizing the contemporary public sphere, we should also consider the well-recognized work of Michael Warner, whose description of the formative influence of circulation in public sphere discourse is worth noting. The first principle he invoked when defining and describing a public is that it is self-organized, functioning as a space of discourse "organized by nothing other than the discourse itself" (Warner, "Abbreviated Version" 50). By "discourse," Warner is referring to a broad set of articulations, including books, Web postings, speeches, and other public statements, as well as visual and audio texts. A codicil to his conception of a public is that it "can only produce a sense of belonging and activity if it is self-organized through discourse rather than through an external framework"

(52). An "external framework" would be an entity like the state or some other enti-
tled institution.

A second principle of Warner's is that a public is the social space created by reflexive circulation of discourse. Warner emphasizes that "a public is understood to be an
ongoing space of encounter for discourse. It is not the circulating texts themselves that
create publics; it is the concatenation of texts through time" (62). Warner's view, then,
is that public discourse is a responding discourse, precipitated and made possible by
discussions that precede it. Thus, the public sphere eventuates from the active circulation of argument about public issues and responses to them.

A third principle articulated by Warner is that "a public is constituted through
mere attention" (60). Warner notes that, unlike other entities, "publics lack any institutional being, commence with the moment of attention, must continually predicate
renewed attention, and cease to exist when attention is no longer predicated" (61).

Manuel Castells' View of the Public Sphere as a Site of Scandal Politics

We will now discuss the aspects of roles played by public controversy and scandal
politics in political campaigns and online news content. In his account of these
developments, Manuel Castells emphasizes the ways in which news releases and
scandal influence public perception of candidates and their policies. He also notes
that these developments operate to capture public attention, an important factor in
public awareness about specific social issues.

In relation to political campaigns, Castells observed that "in the United States,
congressional and state elections typically attract little voter interest, and voters have
scant knowledge about the names of their representatives or their challengers"
(250). He was particularly concerned about the phenomenon of attack politics, or
what he labeled "scandal politics." In tracing patterns of media coverage in political campaigns, Castells noted, "A growing body of research suggests that, for
these politicians, particularly during primaries, being implicated in scandal may actually be beneficial" (250–51). On the other hand, for major political candidates
known to the public, scandals may often prove to be detrimental, because voters
already have information about the candidate and therefore are more inclined to follow the details of the scandal itself.

This phenomenon could be seen during a major scandal that arose during
Barack Obama's presidential campaign in 2008, when videos of his pastor—
Reverend Jeremiah Wright of Trinity Church where Obama was a member—were
widely circulated. Wright was shown on national television in March 2008 expressing extreme views related to race in America. This exposure caused consternation

among Obama's supporters and members of the general public, therefore galvaniz-ing attention to the scandal because candidate Obama was already well known and recognized as a promising candidate.

The outcome of these events and responses to Obama's subsequent speech, "A More Perfect Union," illustrate the significance of a third principle articulated by Warner—that "publics act historically according to the temporality of their circula-tion" ("Abbreviated Version" 68). Warner notes that publics can only act within the temporality of the circulation of discourse that causes them to form. He maintains that "the more punctual and abbreviated the circulation, the more discourse indexes the punctuality of its own circulation and…the closer it stands to politics" (68).

The distribution of controversy and conflict relevant to a scandal is therefore set within the context of its media environment and other attention-getting events, and, as Warner noted, "In modernity, politics takes much of its character from the temporality of the headline, not the archive" (68).

Observers of events prior to and after Barack Obama's "A More Perfect Union" speech concerning Reverend Wright have noted that the pre-speech controversy precipitated by the televised video clips of Wright speaking on race was made available in airings by nearly every major news outlet. Robert Terrill has noted that the clip's circulation on the Internet dwarfed previous controversies "by several orders of magnitude" (366).

The positive impact of the speech given by Obama was so evident, however, that favorable response to it seemed to quell the controversy surrounding his rela-tionship to Wright and his views on race. The speech was widely praised by friends and foes alike, including Hillary Clinton, John McCain, Condoleezza Rice, Colin Powell, and Newt Gingrich. A CBS news poll conducted two nights after the speech indicated that 69% of those who read or saw the speech felt that Obama "did a good job" of addressing race relations, and 70% of registered voters who responded said that recent events (i.e., the scandal) had made no difference in their voting deci-sion (CBS News,"Poll").

By May 30, 2008, the speech had been accessed on YouTube 4.5 million times (CBS News, "Poll"). Its widespread dissemination contributed to its impact. What we learn from these developments is that the scandal triggered by airing and wide-spread circulation of the Wright videos was promptly addressed via Obama's effec-tive and favorably reviewed speech. Its positive reception by a seemingly receptive audience appeared to redirect public attention from the scandal to other develop-ments on the political scene. The timing of developments in this scandal and the public response to it also nicely illustrate Warner's point that publics act within the temporality of the circulation of discourse that causes them to form. In the interim between disclosure of the Wright videos, media and public consternation about them, and Obama's crafted and effective speech, a major disruption in the presidential campaign arose, expanded, and then receded because of the public's favorable reaction to Obama's speech to the nation on the topic of race.

Castells on Mass Self-Communication

The Wright incident just described is an example of what Castells has labeled "scandal politics." In his recent book, *Communication Power*, Castells described specific developments in public and online communication that he viewed as relatively dysfunctional. He observed that "with the diffusion of the internet, a new form of interactive communication has emerged" (55), and he labels this phenomenon as "*mass self-communication*" (66). He notes that what differentiates it from prior forms of mass communication are its methods of production (it is self-generated), its view of potential receivers (which is self-directed), and its patterns of retrieval of content from the World Wide Web (which are self-selected).

The nature of this seemingly solipsistic form of communication seems to be of concern to Castells. Blogs as a form of self-expression would be one example. After noting that a Pew Internet and American Life project reported that 52% of bloggers say that they blog mostly for themselves (Lenhart and Fox), Castells observed that "*a significant share of mass self-communication is closer to "electronic autism" than to actual communication*"(66; emphasis in original).

While in some sense Castells' indictment of blogging is of interest, he is speaking here about personal rather than corporate or news blogs. There are many types of blogs. These include (but are not limited to) personal blogs, which resemble a personal diary or commentary; corporate and individual blogs used for business purposes; and news blogs used to provide analysis and commentary on public issues. Also, many mainstream journalists write their own blogs; some of these are highly regarded sources of information and news (Wikimedia Foundation).

It would seem that, for Castells, "actual" communication is "the sharing of meaning through exchange of information" (54), and presumably, social networking would not necessarily be included in his category of "actual" communication. He acknowledged, nonetheless, that 40% of users having a profile on a social networking site reported that they have used their site for political activity of some kind (390).

Public Inattentiveness and the Role of Infotainment

Castells has been no more sanguine about the nature of mediated politics than he has been about forms of political communication online. His initial concern is about the public's pattern of seeming inattentiveness to political news and issues. He notes that "political messages must overcome a major difficulty to reach the minds of citizens" (205). He cites reports based on information-processing research that indicates that"average Americans pay close attention only to news about significant topics that clearly relate to their lives and experiences" (205). For example, political news that seemed to be of interest to the public at the onset of the midterm election period in 2010 was news that directly affected peoples' lives and well-being. This included the expanding deficit, unemployment, health care reform, increased taxes, and other issues directly related to their well-being. Since much political news is viewed as peripheral information and is often too complex for citizens to attend to and process, it must, in Castells' view, be presented as infotainment. Incidences of infotainment personalize the news in the form of a favorite political figure in ways to which the receiver can relate, and thus are more easily understood and remembered (205).

In addition to the prevalence of infotainment in political reporting, Castells also emphasized the role of scandal politics (such as was seen in the Wright-Obama scandal). Castells noted, "Scandal politics is inseparable from media politics" (249), partly because "the characteristics of media politics make the use of scandals the most effective tool in political contests" (249).

Castells viewed this as due to the personalization of politics. By "personalization," he meant the tendency of media news to focus on the personality and characteristics of a particular political figure so as to relate more readily to the receiver's emotions and interests. He characterizes the ultimate goal of scandal politics as an effort to destroy a political leader by leaking or propagating scandalous behavior that can be attributed to that person. Attack politics as was illustrated in the Reverend Wright scandal is pervasive during highly contested political campaigns. This is due to the fact, pointed out by Castells, that "negative images have a more powerful effect on voting behavior than positive images" (238).

Various strategies are used in attack politics, and these include deployment of negative stereotypes associated with the candidate, distortion of the candidate's policy positions, and accusation of guilt by association, as was effectively illustrated in an incident during the pre-midterm election season in the state of Pennsylvania in July 2010. During that month, the U.S. Chamber of Commerce posted an attack ad directed against second-term Pennsylvania congressman Joe Sestak, who was running for a Senate seat against former Republican congressman Pat Toomey. The ad as initially posted claimed that Sestak "voted with Nancy Pelosi 100 percent of the time" (O'Toole).

Prior video statements by Sestak in the form of video clips showed him supporting government-run health care, cap and trade legislation on emissions, and the $787 billion stimulus measure. The Sestak campaign protested that the "100 percent" claim was inaccurate and asked that television stations withdraw the ad. Two Pittsburgh stations—WPGH and WPMY—pulled their ads for a day. After a meeting with Chamber officials the next day, however, the ad was reinstated after a minor alteration in the ad content that stipulated the precise timeframe of Sestak's voting pattern (Malloy). In the aftermath of the controversy, each campaign's representatives made efforts to impugn the credibility of other.

Online Activism and Offline Results—Spain, 2004

Despite his skepticism about the potential effects of citizen disinterest, politicians' opportunism, and questionable practices in campaigns and other public-sphere activities, Castells nonetheless has appreciated the Internet's capacity to incite online mobilization toward offline actions. Citing research findings that informational media use encourages citizen communication and incites civic engagement, Castells recognizes that at times the Web provides a resource and a forum that eventuates in offline activity and mobilization.

Castells presents a salient example of this phenomenon in his book *Communication Power* that is related to citizen protests in Madrid and Barcelona, Spain following terrorists' simultaneous attacks on four commuter trains in Madrid in March 2004. While José Maria Aznar, then the conservative leader of the country, blamed the Basque terrorist group, ETA, for the bombing, there was widespread suspicion that the culprits were actually connected to Al Qaeda, whose motivation could have been in reaction to Aznar's party's decision to support then President Bush's war in Iraq. Castells surmises that Aznar was motivated to deflect attention to the ETA, because, if the Basques were held responsible, support for the ruling party in the forthcoming election would be bolstered. On the other hand, if the terrorists were from Al Qaeda, its involvement would lead the public to decrease support for Aznar's ruling party, since his party's decisions would be viewed as having precipitated the attack.

On March 12, two days before the scheduled election, the ruling Aznar government was still withholding the information that Al Qaeda was culpable, and police findings were only beginning to reach the public. On March 13, when no political demonstrations were allowed, the government media were still not divulging the facts. Someone (a thirty-year-old educated male) sent out a 160-character SMS message calling on ten friends to gather in front of the ruling party's headquarters at an appointed time, and also to pass on the message to ten more friends (Castells 354). According to Castells, these ten friends forwarded the message to their ten friends, who did the same. The message was also relayed by e-mail and SMS. SMS traffic increased in Spain by 30% over an average Saturday. Castells reported that by shortly after 6 P.M. on March 13, the crowd in front of the ruling party's headquarters had grown to more than 5,000 people. They were shouting,

"Before voting, we want the truth!"and "Liars! Liars! Tomorrow we'll vote; tomorrow we'll throw you out!" (355).

In the subsequent election on the following day, the ruling party (Aznar's) received only 37.6% of the vote, while the Socialist Party received 42.6%. Using an analysis of a number of factors in the voting patterns, Castells concluded that the demonstration on March 13 had an effect on the election outcome, and he also concluded that "a typical instant mobilization phenomenon prompted by a massive network of SMSs" greatly increased the effect of communication through interpersonal channels" (361). This dramatic outcome illustrates the potential of Internet-based political activism to trigger offline results in high-stakes situations and presages other examples of online action that are worth consideration.

Politics Beyond the Public Sphere

Though the examples above illustrate how some Internet discourse might be understood in relationship to theories of the public sphere, not all Web-based political activity falls neatly into traditional conceptions of rational deliberation and reflexivity. Though many online groups may function as an engaged collective, not all will fit an understanding of the traditional public sphere as one that is articulated, bounded, or self-organized. A wide range of activities ranging from oppositional blogging or culture jamming to hacktivism and flash mobs all potentially function through modes of address quite distinct from those discussed thus far. To consider the significance of these kinds of actions, it is necessary to expand our understanding of the public sphere in order to better account for the full scope of online political activity.

Furthermore, it is also important to recognize those online political activities that may be the work of individuals, loosely affiliated or anonymous groups, or parties that may not traditionally be considered political at all. As the Web has grown in popularity, geography has become increasingly less relevant; distinctions between public and private have been blurred, and the norms of deliberation have had to adjust for digital contexts. Because of these and other mitigating factors, existing models of the public sphere must be reconsidered in light of both technological and cultural changes.

Counterpublics

One way of thinking about those groups whose actions might fall outside the scope of the public sphere is to consider the concept of counterpublics. If, according to a traditional Habermasian view, an ideal public sphere is formed around principles of consensus, rationality, and equality, then a counterpublic is formed around principles of disagreement, practicality, and division. In this way, counterpublics can be understood as a coming together of those individuals, ideas, and discursive "exclusions" that cannot or do not circulate within a particular dominant public sphere.

Over the last twenty years this concept of a counterpublic has been defined, redefined, and applied to a number of different contexts. Trying to trace the various uses of the term can seem daunting or, as Kent Ono has suggested, "counterpublic sphere theory…may have a tendency to appear isolating, part of an internal conversation within rhetorical and argumentation studies" (64).[2] However, by working to understand some of the theoretical distinctions that are in play when analyzing counterpublics, we better understand the breadth of political activity that takes place in our culture. Toward that end, it makes sense to start with some of the same critics mentioned earlier in this chapter who pointed out limitations in a Habermasian theory of the public sphere. Many of these scholars were also some of the first to suggest that certain groups of political actors might better be defined as not belonging to a public sphere at all but rather to a counterpublic.

For example, in a 1990 essay Nancy Fraser points to the early twentieth-century feminist movement as a group that functioned as a "subaltern counterpublic"[3] engaged in political activity in "parallel discursive arenas where members of subordinated social groups invent and circulate counterdiscourses, which in turn permit them to formulate oppositional interpretations of their identities, interests, and needs"(67). Fraser uses the example of early feminists because at that time they were unable to participate in the mainstream, male-dominated political system that excluded them. By explaining that they operate in a parallel discursive arena, Fraser suggests that many of the same activities and processes that occur in a Habermasian public sphere also occur in a counterpublic sphere. Furthermore, these counterpublics offered a place for self-definition and expression against any dominant public sphere. And though there are parallels between the spheres, it is important to note the norms of deliberation and reason found in counterpublics are usually not reflective of those found in what Fraser refers to as the broader "multiplicity of publics" (69).

According to Fraser, counterpublics are often "formed under conditions of dominance and subordination" (70) and serve two important functions for their members who have been at least partially excluded from the dominant public sphere. First, they are "spaces of withdrawal and regroupment" (68). That is, they are places where individuals whose discursive practices have been deemed aberrant might find common ground with others who have encountered similar prejudice, persecution, or alienation. In this way, counterpublics provide an audience for ideas that may otherwise never be heard. Fraser considers the early feminist movement as an example par excellence of the counterpublic because their beliefs about the role of women in all strata of society were not a part of the national political conversation. Their continued persistence eventually provided both political change and the creation of an identifiable "space" for feminist discourse that attracted those who shared their convictions.

Second, counterpublics are "bases and training grounds for agitational activities directed toward wider publics" (Fraser 68). For Fraser, counterpublics can be recognized when they engage other, broader publics directly. "Activities" here is vaguely defined, and she acknowledges "that some [counterpublics], alas, are explicitly anti-democratic and anti-egalitarian" (67). Fraser says little about what agitational activities take place within or as a result of counterpublics, but a quick study of the history of social and political movements suggests that counterpublics are bases for both decorous and indecorous political action. Extrapolating, some counterpublic activities are seen as appropriate within a broader political paradigm (e.g., in the United States, sit-ins, marches, and rallies are all widely accepted forms of public protest), while others could be seen as radical or illegal (e.g., property damage or theft, stunts, etc.). For Fraser, then, the term "counterpublic" applies broadly to antagonistic, radical, or otherwise confrontational groups of political actors; under her criteria many groups who have either suffered persecution or engaged in radical protest could be potentially labeled a counterpublic. Historical examples might include groups such as the Black Panthers, women's suffragists, abolitionists, anarchists, the Zapatistas, hippies, teamsters, or LGBT groups.

A more recent example of a group the Fraser might consider to be a counterpublic would be users of Wikileaks.com, a Web site founded in late 2006 to "fight in the legal and political spheres for the broader principles on which our work is based: the integrity of our common historical record and the rights of all peoples to create new history" (Wikileaks). As the name suggests, Wikileaks was created as a Web site for publishing leaked government and corporate information via an online wiki. Any person or group who has confidential information it wants to anonymously make public can submit documents, video, or other media to the wiki for consideration by those who run the site. If the information is deemed noteworthy and credible, it will get published via methods that allow for legal, jurisdictional, and digital protection. As the site's founder Julian Assange suggested in a podcast for BBC's The World, "We're in an arms race…as the data collection increases, we are also increasing our abilities" (PRI's The World). One reason that Fraser's assessment of counterpublics applies to Wikileaks is because they produce and publicize discourses that are deviant from those that traditionally appear in any dominant public sphere. Furthermore, by using a system of open and anonymous sharing to circulate sensitive information, the group runs counter to the conventions of editorial oversight that usually precedes the release of news.

In the summer of 2010, Wikileaks caught the attention of mainstream news outlets when it released more than 90,000 secret military documents related to U.S. actions in Afghanistan. Many of these documents had previously been available to select press outlets, but other documents—including documents detailing strategies for gaining intelligence and documents revealing informant names—contained especially sensitive materials that had been kept from public record. Whereas a more traditional model of public deliberation would suggest that sensitive information should be carefully edited and screened before public dissemination, the loose organization of journalists and programmers who operate Wikileaks chose to publish this information in a digital space that allows for the full details of the document to be read. Wikileaks is a useful example because it fits Fraser's conception of a counterpublic in that the group "emerge[s] in response to exclusions within dominant publics, [and] they help expand discursive space" (67).

In the years following Fraser's essay, much of the scholarship on counterpublics focused on identifying particular groups that could be identified and studied as such.[4] In 2000, Robert Asen published an essay questioning the value of this scholarship. Instead, he argued that the focus of counterpublic scholarship should shift away from identifying a multiplicity of counterpublics by their material makeup (e.g., as groups of "subalterns") and toward identification through "participants recognition of exclusion from wider public spheres and its articulation through alternate discourse practices and norms" (Asen 427). Asen's proposal was essentially that critics should move away from creating broad definitions of publics or counterpublics since the conditions of emergence for either sphere were always discursive and contextual. Asen's essay represented an important shift in counterpublic sphere theory as it allowed scholars with different observations and analyses of counterpublics to potentially reconcile their disparities by effacing binary distinctions between groups.

Michael Warner has also written extensively about the notion of counterpublics, explaining, as did Asen, that they can best be defined in and against those dominant publics that shape much of political and cultural life. Concerned with the potentially broad scope offered by Fraser's definition, Warner specified counterpublics to be those groups that "maintain at some level, conscious or not, an awareness of [their] subordinate status....Fundamentally mediated by public forms, counterpublics incorporate the personal/impersonal address and expansive estrangement of public speech as the condition of their own common world" ("Abbreviated Version" 86–87). Like Fraser and Asen, he acknowledged the temporal situatedness and the variant circulation of discourse in counterpublics, but he was not willing to suggest that these characteristics necessarily retain an oppositional character for the duration of a group's political life.

Much of Warner's writing was focused on how counterpublics could find a means of obtaining agency and voice in broader political arenas, and he studied how structuring discourses change over time to allow for this to happen. In fact, because of the close relationship with the very publics they are counter to (counterpublics are "constituted through a conflictual relation to the dominant public" ["Publics and Counterpublics" 423]), Warner suggested that for many counterpublics the moment of political agency coincided with the moment of co-optation into a broader public. Counterpublics stop being "counter" when they are acknowledged. In fact, for a counterpublic to persist, it must "make no attempt" (423) to ever present itself as "the public." This limits the kind of political goals and tactics available to a counterpublic. Warner further explained that "a public of subalterns is only a counterpublic when its participants are addressed in a counterpublic way" and "in some cases, such as fundamentalism…participants are not subalterns for any reason other than their participation in counterpublic discourse" (424).

The contemporary Tea Party movement is an instructive example of a briefly viable counterpublic that lost its status as such and gained agency when recognized as a legitimate part of broader national political deliberation. Though it emerged publicly in early 2009, *Huffington Post* reporter Alex Brant-Zawadzki places the origins of the movement early in the middle of the 2008 presidential campaign, in December 2007. According to Brant-Zawadzki's timeline, the movement's inception was based on people uniting behind a set of related ideas that emerged across select blogs, political conference speeches, viral videos on the Web, and some conservative talk-radio programs. Although this consensus certainly reflected a right-wing ideology, it was an ideology that did not fit neatly into any existing conservative political party platform. In brief, at its beginning the Tea Party movement was solely invested in cutting government spending, limiting government involvement in social programs, and holding existing members of Congress responsible for their actions. Influenced by politicians such as Ron Paul, the movement had a strong libertarian and independent streak and sought the kind of wholesale reform in government that would disrupt the existing two-party dynamic.

In other words, even if the ideas and activities of the Tea Party movement were not entirely new (and certainly not radical), they were, as Warner suggests, in a "conflictual relationship" to mainstream political discourses. Members loudly disrupted local town hall meetings concerning healthcare, held small protests in targeted voting districts, mailed tea bags to members of Congress, and engaged in other forms of unorthodox protest. For a brief period of time they maintained antagonism toward both Republicans and Democrats and during this period could be classified as a counterpublic by both Fraser and Warner's definitions. However, a quick series of events in late 2009 and early 2010 led to the movement's eventual co-optation and incorporation into mainstream party discourses.

First, starting with some of their earliest protests, the Tea Party began to court sympathetic elected officials from the Republican Party. For example, at some of their mid-summer protests, Tea Partyers engaged in a call and response with members of the House in front of the capitol lawn. They later invited these Republicans to speak at Tea Party events and rallies. Continuing into 2010, the Tea Party claimed responsibility for the election of Republican Senator Scott Brown in Massachusetts and Rand Paul's victory in the Kentucky U.S. Senate Republican primary. The first Tea Party caucus, held in July, was chaired by Republican Representative Michele Bachmann (Brant-Zawadzki). Collectively, this continued courting of mainstream Republican Party officials helped to promote the Tea Party's agenda onto the Republican Party platform and into mainstream political discourse.

Concurrently, the Tea Party movement gained increased national exposure and support from Fox News and some of its popular personalities. Several Tea Party events were heavily covered and promoted on the Fox News channel in the spring and summer of 2009, and as its popularity grew, the movement gained wider cultural capital. For example, a Media Matters report indicates that the nationwide April 15, 2009, Tea Party Tax Day event was basically co-sponsored by Fox News and many of its hosts. In their special report they explain that the coverage served as a recruitment tool: "Fox News has frequently aired segments encouraging viewers to get involved with 'tea party' protests across the country, which the channel has described as primarily a response to President Obama's fiscal policies"(H., E.H.). Fox's coverage emphasized the strength of a united national movement and omitted mention of many of the localized and/or guerilla tactics found in the earliest days of the Tea Party movement. By downplaying these more radical forms of political engagement, Fox News also played a role in repositioning the movement from one that was counter to and opposed to mainstream politics to one that could have a legitimate political voice in the public sphere.[5]

Through these two developments, the Tea Party lost its status as a counterpublic that, according to Warner, often consists of ordinary people who "are presumed not to want to be mistaken for the kind of person that would participate in this kind of talk, or to be present in this kind of scene" ("Publics and Counterpublics" 424). Warner's emphasis on the connections between the public, counterpublics, and agency highlights the significant role that visibility plays in understanding how political discourse gets legitimized. By building on the scholarship of people such as Fraser and Asen, Warner offers one of the most nuanced understandings of counterpublics to date.

Because of this, Warner's work on counterpublics was the focus of a 2002 issue of the *Quarterly Journal of Speech*. In that issue, David Wittenberg critiqued Warner's conception of the counterpublic by calling into question the aforementioned theories of space and visibility utilized in Warner's work. Wittenberg noted the slippage in Warner's use of this term ("discursive space," "social space," etc.) and recognized that Warner's public "abstracts itself out of space" (428). Instead, Wittenberg invoked Kierkegaard's writing about publicity[6] to remind us that a group's appearance in the public is a victory with consequences as there is "the danger of being removed from the public, not (necessarily) by being disappeared, but precisely by being made to appear too much" (432). Wittenberg thus pushed Warner to his teleological end: what happens to a counterpublic after it achieves agency and is subsumed into the public sphere? This question of appearance is a very real one for activisms grounded in the digital contexts of cyberspace where successful activism often relies on strategic presencing.[7]

Strangers and Outlaws

As we've seen, the notion of a counterpublic can be useful for defining and analyzing certain groups in and against a rational-critical Habermasian framework. However, the complexity of both public sphere and counterpublic sphere theory often makes either concept less than accessible to the study of many real-world cases. One method for circumventing the potential confusion that occurs when navigating these competing theoretical positions is to search for alternative conceptual frameworks. In other words, there are other useful techniques for critiquing how political discourses circulate, shape personal identity, and effect change beyond those provided in the public-counterpublic literature. Many of these alternatives take into consideration the debate above, using it as a jumping-off point for considering those groups and individuals whose political and personal value is difficult to ascertain through either model of the public. Since the focus of this project is on the application of rhetorical theory and criticism to Web-based politics, it is worth briefly considering some of these other critical perspectives.

One such perspective was offered in the very same issue of the *Quarterly Journal of Speech* that investigated Warner's counterpublics. In an article that focused on the kinds of indecorous discourses that marked Warner's counterpublics, Melissa Deem challenged some of the basic assumptions of the public-counterpublic binary. Specifically, she demonstrated how publics and counterpublics alike were able to bring strangers together through processes of socialization and suggested that the earliest discursive processes in group formation were "particularly crucial" to understanding how groups attain or lose agency (Deem 445). That is, Deem contended that it is not critical-rational discourse that structured power in Warner's counterpublics but rather indecorous acts that spread throughout the group early on that "open up the possibilities for oppositional or transformative practice" (446).

Therefore, Deem proposed that critics might turn to the analysis of those key indecorous discourses (or what she calls "minor rhetorics") present at the inception of a political movement. She writes:

> An understanding of minor rhetorics, through the concept of decorum, is central to an
> understanding of the logics that are mechanisms of containment and exclusion within
> political discourse...[and] of the ways in which minor rhetorics dislodge the discursive
> foundation of the political. (448)

When applying this concept to the Web, minor rhetorics might be found in those posts left on Web site message boards, blog comments sections, Facebook pages, or other Web-based forums where much of a movement's early Web activity takes place.

For example, the Web site 4chan.org has conducted a number of both Web-based and public protests over the years operating under the pseudonym of "Anonymous." Their ongoing campaign against the Church of Scientology is perhaps their most famous activity, though they have also campaigned against the Australian government, Iranian elections, and other global political causes.[8] Despite the apparent cohesiveness found in these activities, the group itself is only loosely organized and affiliated via ongoing and anonymous activity on the 4chan message boards. On those boards, much of the activity takes the form of "minor rhetorics" in that they "use the language of the majority in such a way as to make that language stutter" (447). Deem's perspective allows us to understand the kind of discussion found on 4chan.org's forums as a site for agency; there we can see the potential for discursively grounded practices to function as a device that continuously displaces the public-counterpublic binary. In 4chan's forums, everyone and no one is "unfit for publicness" (449).

Less concerned with a movement's inception or lifecycle than Deem or Warner, Kent Ono and John Sloop offer an approach to studying movements that focuses on issues of identity construction and on the rhetorical modes of persistence, appearance, and disappearance found in groups outside of the political or cultural mainstream. With a concentration on smaller communities and nonparticipant politics, Ono and Sloop have presented a critical approach for studying what they refer to as vernacular ("Critique of Vernacular Discourse") and outlaw discourses ("Outlaw Discourse").

Ono and Sloop's conception of outlaw discourses is especially appealing for a study of Web community–based activism, as the strategies they focus on are typical of much of online discursive activity. They explain:

> We see outlaw discourses as loosely shared logics of judgment and procedure for liti-
> gation....Outlaw discourse communities posit their sense of justice as one that should
> properly be shared by the dominant community. ("Outlaw Discourse," 51)

Outlaw discourses have implications for identity in that they "concern judgments made in the practice of everyday life" (60) and are deployed by "a being or group [to] preserve its identity—either through the creation of new ways to understand experiences…or through physical force" (63).

The theory of outlaw discourses is closely tied to Ono and Sloop's earlier work, "The Critique of Vernacular Discourse," which places "an emphasis on continuous discursive displacement…a critique of vernacular discourse strives to understand how a community is constructed and how that constructed community functions" ("Critique" 25–26). Important to their project was a theory of conditional essentialism, which allows for groups to operate in a metonymic fashion as the situation around them dictates.

Hacktivist groups, those engaged in acts of hacking for political purposes, are an example of a group that might be productively analyzed using the perspective offered by Ono and Sloop. For one, hacktivists frequently demonstrate conditional essentialism by choosing how to invoke core hacktivist values, such as the hacker ethic, in a variety of situations. In order to justify their actions, these values are continually reframed and renegotiated for contemporary concerns. This is also true of groups such as the 9/11 "Truthers," who must always reframe their arguments about the supposed government conspiracies behind the events of September 11, 2001, in light of new evidence that calls their claims into question. Both hacktivists and Truthers are examples of groups who have learned how to effectively use rhetorical techniques of appearance, disappearance, and metonymy in digital contexts so as to persist as loosely affiliated and antagonistic communities.

For Ono and Sloop, the critic should champion marginalized culture and subculture, and they suggest that rhetorical critics might bring these discourses into the public imaginary, giving them attention through critique and "highlight the logics of particular outlaw judgments" ("Outlaw Discourse," 64). In fact, rhetoricians are "uniquely positioned" to do this due to their "materialist[ic] conception of judgment" (54). And though Ono and Sloop acknowledge the limiting potential in setting up this dialogic model, the critical move is itself justified as a form of strategic essentialism.[9]

An Overview of New Media Research

Thus far we have focused on those ongoing shifts in public deliberation and debate that we take to be of central significance in both offline and online contemporary politics. By explaining the significance of public-sphere theory, counterpublics, and other perspectives for understanding the rhetorical processes that accompany these shifts, we have offered an overview that indicates much of our own scholarly background for studying politics online. However, critical scholarship on new media is increasingly diverse and interdisciplinary, and this book also touches on work done in media studies, critical cultural studies, English and composition, other areas of communication studies, and related disciplines. This chapter concludes with several examples of how this research connects with our own interests in studying the relationship between political transformations and new media technologies.

New Media Research in Media Studies: Mary Chayko on Mobile Technology

Some of the most interesting and innovative scholarship addressing Web-based politics is done in media studies, a field that employs a wide range of perspectives and methodologies. Inclusive of everything from ongoing longitudinal studies focusing on how people use the Web for both personal and political reasons[10] to critical-historical scholarship that reads the Web against the cultural history of other technologies,[11] media studies offers a wealth of material for better understanding how the Web has increasingly shaped human interaction. Like the study of rhetoric, the study of media encompasses a range of various disciplines that each offer a different component to the nuanced field. And like rhetorical criticism, media studies is well suited to tackle some of the most important questions about the growth of digital technologies.

Mary Chayko's *Portable Communities: The Social Dynamics of Online and Mobile Connectedness* (2008) is exemplary of how this mixed methodological, cross-disciplinary focus applies to the study of some of the more intriguing aspects of new media technologies. In her study of social networking, mobile device usage, and other recent ICTs, Chayko starts from the position that "as a sociologist with a background in communication and psychology, there is little [about new media communication technologies] that I do not think interesting or important" (*Portable Communities* 5). Like many media studies scholars, she studies the field from a particular disciplinary perspective (sociology) and in the process both extends the scope of sociology and adds to the investigative depth of media studies.

Chayko offers several examples and case studies that are productive for considering how new media shapes community. In her discussion of how people get involved in communities she cites MMO playing, online gambling, social networking, and other forms of online activity as activities that are "so seductive, easy, and so much fun to go online…we (and our children) may indeed become immersed, even engulfed, in behaviors" (85) that are potentially destructive to other areas of one's life. Part of this allure, she explains, is the usage of "playful talk" such as gossiping, flirting, and joking that can be found in many mobile communities and that "promote and bring about social bonding, on and offline" (77). Because of the hypertextual and connected quality of the Web, these kinds of activities, which mark much of users' online experiences in communities across the Internet, are frequently carried over to those areas of the Web where we see forms of political engagement. The ubiquity of "play" across the Web cannot be underestimated when considering any Web site, no matter how "serious" it portends to be.

Chayko also points to the voyeuristic nature of many of the online interactions that users engage in within their Web-based communities. The anonymous nature of Web usage allows for members to feel that they belong to a community without ever engaging in member-to-member interaction, to observe without being identified, and in some cases to contribute without the consequence of any kind of self-disclosure. Pointing to activities such as lurking, Chayko explains that

> when we peek in on what others are doing online, we gain a sense of exactly who comprises our portable communities—what they are doing and what they think about and, most importantly, who they are as individuals and as a collective....We need to feel the presence of others in our networks and communities and to be present to them in return. Lurking helps us to feel another's presence. (175)

This behavior is not limited to Web surfing while sitting at a PC, and Chayko found that (especially younger) ICT users engaged in various mobile forms of both identity building and the social surveillance of others. "There is every reason to believe that upcoming generations of online and mobile connectors will find much of this neither daunting or confusing" as those who grow up using these technologies have "skills in accessing information, interacting, and building social worlds online, in multitasking and moving unproblematically between social spheres, and in considering what occurs in sociomental space to be very much 'real'" (180).

Once again, these observations about online behavior and demographics are important for rhetoricians to consider when thinking about the habits of interaction and the capabilities of particular audiences to respond to a rhetor. The field's emphasis on contextual frames of analysis means that media studies investigates many of the same questions that interest rhetoricians, and a better understanding of their methods and perspectives can enrich rhetorical criticism of new media.

New Media Research in English: Jamie Skye Bianco on the Rhetoric of Security on Facebook and Other Sites

In an article in *Women's Studies Quarterly* in 2009, Jamie Skye Bianco traced developments related to cloud computing and personal privacy online. She began by observing that whereas with Web 2.0 software, users were dealing with content they had developed and posted and over which they had control; more recently users are relying on cloud computing that is an outgrowth of Web 2.0. With cloud computing, content is stored on networked-based applications that house the user's data. Under this system, both the program and any user documents and data reside on the host's networked server and *not* on the user's hard drive (Bianco, p. 303).

This means that the host network (be it Facebook, MySpace, Flickr, YouTube, Google, or other networking sites) is in possession of the user's data and has some control over its distribution. Bianco describes the technological and corporate environment in which privacy and security issues are handled and explained to users. She notes, in regard to her observations that the platforms and communicative capacities mentioned here just scratch the surface of the complexities of self-production and distribution, sharing, networking, and community organizing that social networking makes available (Bianco, p. 304).

To illustrate the potentiality that such sites have for disseminating significant and just-in-time information, Bianco describes the experiences of Janis Krums on 15 January 2009. He was leaving New York City and boarded a ferry to cross the Hudson River at 3:36 P.M. Soon thereafter, he posted a "tweet," or microblogged message post, on Twitter. He reported that he could see a plane in the Hudson River. (It was U.S. Airways Flight 1549, which had made an emergency landing when the plane was damaged after takeoff.) A picture of the crippled plane was taken by Krums who uploaded it to Twitpic. Within less than half an hour, Krums was interviewed live on MSNBC. Bianco cites this saga as an example of citizen journalism made possible by the capability of digital recording technologies, microblogging services, and other portable recording devices.

Bianco goes on to note that these conveniences are not without their downsides, however. She then scrutinizes the practices implemented by social-networking sites such as Facebook, MySpace, Flickr, and YouTube. These entities provide a service to users who enjoy them at low cost and with little effort. Nevertheless, it is worth noting that such online sites provide storage and dissemination capacity and do need to monetize their traffic by using their resources, including their users' data and information. Bianco points out that, while Facebook gained in popularity because of the perception that its primary practices and closed networking countered MySpace's exposures, Facebook in fact had a rather ambiguous license agreement. Bianco cited the 2009 version of Facebook's end-user license agreement:

> Profile information is used by Facebook *primarily* to be presented back to and edited by you when you access the service and to be presented to others permitted to view that information by your privacy settings....Facebook may use information in your profile without identifying you as an individual to third parties.... *We believe this benefits you.* (Bianco, p. 306, emphasis added)

The third parties, of course, would be advertisers and patrons of the site in question. Bianco expresses skepticism that users will be able to distinguish between targeted marketing efforts and the latest "share with your friends" meme circulating on the Facebook network. Furthermore, they may be unlikely to recognize that third-party applications fully access the user's data and do not provide the same caveats and provisos as Facebook's terms of service.

Bianco's article was published in 2009, but consulting Facebook's privacy policy in 2010 indicates that the situation has improved, although it still retains many of the features that she pointed out. The current terms of service as of April 22, 2010, explained to users that the site uses tracking capability to document site activity (e.g., creating a photo album, sending a gift, sharing a video), and they might also log user actions such as sharing that video. They also note that data sharing, commonly known as "conversion tracking," helps Facebook to measure its advertising effectiveness and improve the quality of the advertisements displayed to users. In addition, the privacy policy includes other codicils that might be of concern to users if those users are aware of their implications. These appear under the "Other" header in the policy and include such aspects as the following:

- You understand that information might be reshared or copied by other users.
- Certain types of communications that you send to other users cannot be removed, such as messages.
- When you post information on another user's profile or comment on another user's post, that information will be subject to the other user's privacy settings ("Facebook's Privacy Policy").

Also, one hopes that Facebook users are aware of the implications of the "Everyone" setting on Facebook, as described in the policy:

> Information sent to "everyone" is publicly available information, just like your name, profile picture, and connections. Such information may, for example, be accessed by everyone on the internet (including people not logged into Facebook), be indexed by third party search engines, and be imported, exported, distributed, and redistributed by us and others without privacy limitations. Such information may also be associated with you, including your name and profile picture, even outside of Facebook, such as on public search engines and when you visit other sites on the internet. *The default privacy setting for certain types of information you post on Facebook is set to "everyone."* You can review and change the default settings in your privacy settings ("Facebook's Privacy Policy," emphasis added).

One hopes that users new to Facebook know that the default privacy setting is "everyone." While Facebook users can control their privacy settings to some extent so as to stipulate who will have access to their content, frequent necessary adjustments by users to their privacy settings may be overlooked and neglected in the course of their social networking activities.

The site statement on shared information is as follows:

> Facebook is about sharing information with others—friends and people in your communities—while providing you with privacy settings that you can use to restrict other users from accessing *some* of your information. We share your information with third parties when we believe the sharing is permitted by you, reasonably necessary to offer our services, or when legally required to do so ("Facebook Privacy Policy," emphasis added).

What might be the ramifications of the last statement? Facebook provides additional information in response to this question:

> We may disclose information pursuant to subpoenas, court orders, or other requests (including criminal and civil matters) if we have a good faith belief that the response is required by law. This may include respecting requests from *jurisdictions outside of the United States* where we have a good faith belief that the response is required by law under the local laws in that jurisdiction, applies to users from that jurisdiction, and is consistent with generally accepted international standards. ("Facebook's Privacy Policy," emphasis added)

How might this play out? In August 2010, a fifteen-year-old adolescent from Pittsburgh was arrested by state authorities in India and accused of killing his mother at a resort and dumping her body at the bottom of a sand dune nearby. Relatives and close friends of the accused young man maintained that he could not have committed such an act. Unfortunately for him, however, there were among the hundreds of posts on his Facebook page references to his mother as "Satan" and "bitch," as well as a statement in 2009 that said "i am going to kill my mom," without any further explanation (Riely). The issues with his mother in August 2010 apparently revolved around where he was to attend school when they returned from their trip and her interference in his relationship with his father.

While it is unclear how his Facebook content was accessed, it is clear that the cited contents of his Facebook posts in regard to his mother were very incriminating. This is just a very clear instance of how someone's posts on a social-networking site can become very problematic for that person later on.

Bianco concludes her article on cloud computing and the security of information with a provocative question. After noting the potential for Google Library and

Google Books projects to use this form of technology to stand alone in digitizing the world's print archives, she wonders whether "there is a serious problem with one company, albeit one whose motto is "Don't do evil," digitally housing and controlling access to the majority of human knowledge production." To place that much content in a computing context potentially subject to system failures and ambiguous policies in regard to the content it controls could be a measure that results in dire consequences.

New Media Research in Critical Cultural Studies: Anne Kustritz on Slash Fan Fiction and Web Communities

Just as media studies scholarship frequently draws on theories originating in disciplines such as sociology, mass communication, philosophy or cultural studies, so too do we in this present study. Scholars as diverse as Stuart Hall, W. J. T. Mitchell, Gilles Deleuze, Jacques Derrida, Guy Debord, Walter Benjamin, James Carey, and Michel Foucault are all cited in the field's literature because of what their theories of language, technology, and space and time offer for the critique of new media texts. With a focus on culture, subculture, race, class, gender, and sexuality, cultural studies offers an abundance of resources for understanding rhetorical processes in new media.

Especially interesting in much of cultural studies scholarship are the many ways in which key concepts and terminology get utilized, debated, and productively (mis)understood. Consider, for example, Anne Kustritz's essay "Slashing the Romance Narrative," which is representative of cultural studies scholarship that draws on some of the foundational figures in the field to illuminate how one particular community of Web users—slash fan fiction communities—operate.[12] In her essay, Kustritz carefully chooses when to strategically invoke the terms "community" or "subculture" to refer to that group of Internet users who regularly write, read, or comment on slash fan fiction. She writes that "until the 1990s, slash remained tucked away, a subculture within a subculture" (372). She then suggests that, with its publication on the Internet, slash fiction was able to appeal to a broader audience. Prior to its "move" to the Web it was a "subculture," afterwards it becomes a "community."[13]

In the essay, Kurstritz details features of the community: demographic information (mostly college-educated and "frustrated" women), aesthetic tastes and standards (e.g., disdain for the certain character stereotypes), and even "community activities" such as creating a fan canon (or "fanon") or issuing "list challenges" to members of particular message boards or listservs. The notion of community is especially important at the end of the essay, when she writes:

> The metatext tells us how to live as a community of women who support, critique, and love each other....These communities are actively involved in constructing a life that is truly worth living....Perhaps it is not the potential to change the world, but it is the potential to change women's lives, one individual, one story, and one day at a time. (Dionne, 383)

The emphasis in the article is on the relationship between personal fulfillment through both slash fan fiction community activities and the establishment of communally developed relationships. Kustritz's focus on slash fan fiction writers as a "community" provides a basis for thinking about the significance of that term, and scholarship with this kind of focus—which is found throughout cultural studies—helps us to think through the distinctions between subcultures, communities, publics, counterpublics, and other forms of rhetorically significant collectives.

Other approaches in cultural studies for studying and naming "community" vary significantly from Kustritz's use of the term. In other words, the choice to describe the slash fan fiction "community" as such implies a self-contained discursive space in which certain forms of civic discourse (as defined by "community standards") prevail. Furthermore, it suggests that any "effects" of community discourse are then limited to members of the community. In addition, as Jodi Dean points out, "Community may well be the most powerful of the aspirations linked to the World Wide Web....It evokes the friendliness of neighbors stopping by for advice or a cup of sugar...in a community, everyone knows your name" (4). Dean suggests that, in contrast to the popular move that Kustritz and other critics make to label certain Web collectives as "communities," critics would be wise to consider how the Web itself has been detrimental to the formation of traditional communities: "Rather than fulfilling community, the Web seems to threaten it as it enables people to play with identities, forfeit responsibilities, and indulge in potentially dangerous fantasies" (13).

Dean's emphasis, then, is on the reasons why Web communities aren't really analogous to traditional real-world communities. By implying that any scholarship equating them is flawed, she prompts a question: if these Web users are not forming "communities," then what are these collections of people with shared interests? Kahn and Kellner suggest an answer to this question with their term "post-subculture." The term "post-subculture" can be used to describe "the new emerging subcultures [that] are taking place in a world that is saturated with media awareness and being propelled into new global configurations by technological advances such as the internet and multimedia" (299). Post-subcultures have more in common with the traditional notion of subculture as described by Dick Hebdige than with any bounded-rational community.[14] They write that "however, as with previous generations of subcultures, internet subcultures are desirous of a certain immediacy of experience that seeks to circumvent dominant codes" (299). Aside from being an apt description of how slash fan fiction fans use the Web, this definition allows for slash fan fiction writers and readers to maintain their identity as members of a subculture who have moved into and utilized a new medium.

The result of this move is not the creation of a "community" from what was once a "subculture" but rather an important territorial shift in an existent and continuing subculture. Rather than sanitizing the truly political nature of the slash writers by using terminology that emphasizes only group dynamics or individual identity, the notion of "post-subculture" posits slash fan fiction writers and readers as subjects directly opposed to the mainstream ideologies, norms, and so forth. Kahn and Kellner again argue that "technoculture makes possible a reconfiguring of politics, a refocusing of politics of everyday life, and the use of tools and techniques of emergent computer and communication technologies to expand the field of politics and culture" (311). To talk about "slash fan fiction post-subcultures" as opposed to "slash fan fiction communities" is to argue that the act of slashing characters from popular science fiction and fantasy has the potential to provoke and persuade others outside of the subculture into changing their own cultural beliefs about homosexual relationships, the politics of male-oriented plots in various forms of entertainment, and so on.

It also opens up the possibility that the act of "slashing" remains a political form of writing and not simply writing for the edification of the "slash community" or the individual. In other words, a post-subculture retains a dialogic relationship with the world, giving it the potential to indeed change more than only "women's lives, one individual, one story, and one day at a time" (Kustritz 383).

This focused attention on the significance and appropriation of critical terminology has an affinity with much of the scholarship in rhetorical criticism, and the field of cultural studies offers us an avenue for considering how and why we choose to frame our own arguments and analysis about the Internet as we look at Web-based culture throughout this book.

New Media Research in Communication Studies: Clay Shirky on the Effects of Social Networking in the Public Sphere

In his well-received book, *Here Comes Everybody*, Clay Shirky emphasizes the role and influence of the growth of social networking on the public sphere. He also notes that when communication on the Internet became rapidly facilitated in the early 2000s, its use decreased transaction costs for businesses as everyday individuals began using the online environment to create groups, mobilize constituencies, publicize issues, and solve problems at no cost other than the use of Internet tools themselves. Shirky maintained that "the transfer of these capabilities from professional classes to the general public is epochal, built on 'an architecture of participation'" (17).

Shirky's book received many favorable reviews, including one by prominent blogger Bruce Schneier who noted, "The book is filled with bits of insight and common sense, explaining why young people take better advantage of social tools, how the internet affects social change, and how most internet discourse falls somewhere between dinnertime conversation and publishing" (Schneier).

Unlike corporations and businesses that operate through a management structure that requires a hierarchical configuration, coordinated and managed activity, and layers of structure and rules, the users of social networks, blogs, and other online tools can work without the managerial imperative and outside previous structures that would have limited their effectiveness. Furthermore, Shirky notes that in this new communication ecology, "the cost of all kinds of group activity—sharing, cooperation, and collective action—have fallen dramatically. Social tools provide an alternative to institutionalized action because they have the capacity to instigate action by loosely structured groups, operating without managerial direction and outside the profit motive" (47).

To illustrate his points, Shirky introduces a number of examples of the use of social networking to address crises, participate in policy formation, and bring major issues into public attention that otherwise would have gone relatively unnoticed. This is particularly vital when governments impose restrictions or institutional resistance blocks public access to signal events. Some of Shirky's examples include notifications made available by London citizens to other citizens at the time of the London transport bombings in 2005, Indymedia's coverage of abuses against citizens in New Orleans after Hurricane Katrina, and coverage of the aftereffects of the Indian Ocean tsunami in December 2004. He notes that when official news media do not have access to developing crises, people with camera phones and Internet access are capable of informing the public of what is happening.

Furthermore, the resources of social networking can, at times, trump the official news media when the media fails to take due notice of a breaking story. Shirky's example here is when Trent Lott, then majority leader in the Senate, praised segregationist Strom Thurman's political stance and professional record at Thurman's birthday party on December 5, 2002. The newspapers initially did not cover this story about Lott's inappropriate remarks. Instead, it was liberal and conservative bloggers who brought the public's attention to the incident, and Lott subsequently announced his intention not to continue in his Senate post. This example illustrates the constraints under which mainstream news outlets work. To be effective, news must have a certain frame that the public can relate to, such as available photographs or video clips depicting the situation being discussed. Since these components were not available within the twenty-four-hour news cycle, the news media neglected to highlight the Lott story until bloggers brought it to the public's attention shortly after Lott's speech was made public.

The kind of media shift described by Shirky can be compared with historical media shifts in which conventional forms of expression were changed because of the advent of new technologies. For example, as Walter J. Ong noted in his book *Orality and Literacy*, the advent of literacy in ancient Greek culture had profound effects on communication practices, cultural preservation, and education during that time. It precipitated the turn to formal logic and the abstraction of knowledge that gradually supplanted the oral epic as a means of preserving culture. Likewise, the shift from hand-copied manuscripts to print books in the sixteenth century had equally profound effects on education and culture. Print enabled mass produced, standardized texts that were repeatable and identical in large quantities. It also facilitated the reproduction of charts and logic tables in educational models of the day, thereby commodifying knowledge. In addition, it introduced standardization into education so that all students were studying and learning the same thing. These were transnational phenomena. Shirky's argument for the profound changes introduced by social networking and blogging is analogous to the historical observations made by Ong.

Shirky notes that the affordances of social networking have enabled "mass amateurization" (98) which has contributed to the loss of the "clear distinctions between communications media and broadcast media" (98). At this point, one important observation of Shirky's should be invoked:

> It's when a technology becomes normal, then ubiquitous, and finally so pervasive as to be invisible, that the really profound changes happen, and for young people today, our new social tools have passed normal and are heading to ubiquitous, and invisible is coming. (105)

To establish his position, Shirky turns to the example of Wikipedia as a collaborative site of content and knowledge production.[15] The history of the Wikipedia enterprise is quite interesting. Originally Jimmy Wales and Larry Sanger founded Wikipedia in 2001 as an experimental offshoot of their original idea, a free online encyclopedia of high quality called Nupedia (109). However, their initial plan of using qualified experts to post assigned articles did not function well. The arrangements made for production of the work turned out to be ineffective and, in fact, were excruciatingly slow. Sanger speculated that a more open process for submitting content would facilitate development of the project. He suggested the Wiki tool (i.e., a user-editable Web site) for getting this done. Shirky notes that this collaborative Wiki tool creates a way for the software community to devise a means of collaboratively storing shared wisdom (111).

To illustrate the functionality of Wikipedia, let us return to the example of the London subway bombing mentioned earlier. When major sites of underground transportation in London were destroyed by terrorist attacks in July 2005, someone initiated a Wikipedia entry within minutes of the event, followed by additional news from other users as time passed. The postings contained helpful information such as links to traditional news sources and contact numbers for people trying to find a way to get home. Shirky describes this set of developments as an example of how Wikipedia (ostensibly an encyclopedia) has exceeded its original purpose and has become a coordinating resource through the in-time information that it can provide.

The effects of profound changes in our communication infrastructure may be best clarified by an additional example provided by Shirky. Here, he provides an account of the Catholic Church's historical efforts to downplay or wait out scandals related to priests' misconduct with their parishioners. When the case of Father John Geoghan, a Catholic priest in the Boston Archdiocese who, over many years, had fondled or raped more than a hundred boys became public, the lay organization of Catholics, Voice of the Faithful, was formed. The group grew in size from thirty people in a church basement to 25,000 members both nationally and internationally during 2002. Shirky noted that, whereas earlier scandals related to priestly abuse had been tamped down and kept relatively quiet by the church in prior years, by 2002 this was no longer possible. Two major developments brought about the change. First, the *Boston Globe* went online as *Boston.com*, and its online readers could then forward stories regarding the abuse scandals to interested parties domestically and internationally very easily. And, of course, those forwarded messages could then be forwarded by their initial recipients to other parties. Shirky concludes:

> In 1992 the *Globe* wasn't global, and the priest abuse story stayed in Boston. In 2002, the *Globe* didn't need to spread the story to the world's Catholics; the Catholics were capable of doing that themselves. (149)

Furthermore, the redistribution of this information incited widespread controversy in the press. Each time some aspect of the controversy recurred, the church's ability to wait out the controversy eroded a little more because the issue became more salient each time it was discussed in the news. This developing situation became and remained prominent in the public eye because it was much more difficult for the Catholic Church to take no action than it had been in prior years.

Shirky concludes his analysis by noting that online social tools remove obstacles to collective action, and as the obstacles are removed, the world is becoming a different place due to the availability of easy-to-use tools like e-mail, mobile phones, and Web sites. He maintains that these changes have happened not because of the tools but because society has adopted new behaviors.

Conclusion

It is our view that the public sphere, as traditionally understood, is in a state of crisis brought on by significant changes in both institutional politics and the forms of discursive activity being taken up by the polis. Significantly, rhetorical uses of new media technologies feature prominently in these changes. In this chapter, we have explained a wide range of recent political activity and the role of new media therein. In doing so, we have highlighted how a variety of perspectives on the public sphere, counterpublics, and other forms of political organizing and action might be understood in and against these political and technological shifts. One goal of this book is to explain how rhetorical criticism can be used to analyze political activity in new media, and by starting with some familiar approaches to thinking about questions of political transformation we have laid that groundwork above.

Studying rhetoric online requires grappling with new technologies and with ongoing changes in how people communicate with one another, form collectives, participate as citizens, and use rhetorical processes to shape a worldview. As we've explained in this chapter, there are a variety of disciplines that offer useful ideas for understanding these processes—we view this project as one with interdisciplinary appeal. In the next chapter we'll focus on a specific U.S. election: the 2010 midterm, to further clarify the benefits of this particular approach to studying the rhetoric of new media.

Notes

1. As noted later in this chapter, sociologist Manuel Castells has documented social networking's lack of attention to public deliberation as revealed in the Pew Internet and American Life Project in 2006. See Lenhart and Fox for documentation of this trend.
2. By "counterpublic sphere theory" Ono refers primarily to that scholarship in rhetorical criticism that considers the practices of groups that run counter to the Habermasian model of public deliberation addressed above. Often, those groups involved in social movements (a traditional focus of rhetorical inquiry) can be categorized in this way.
3. Fraser borrows the term "subaltern" from Gayatri Spivak. Spivak suggested in her famous essay "Can the Subaltern Speak?" that "subaltern" is a word that refers to "men and women among the illiterate peasantry, the tribals, the lowest strata of the urban subproletariat" (25) who are the "'true' subaltern group, whose identity is its difference" (27). In her use of the term, Spivak refers specifically to those groups who are the subject of much postcolonial scholarship.
4. See, for example, Maguire and Mohtar's 1994 study of a community women's center.
5. It could be argued that the Tea Party's political stance against taxation helps bolster the bottom line of media conglomerates like Fox News Corp.

6. Wittenberg bases his discussion on Kierkegaard's well-known practice of writing under pseudonyms and avoiding publicity. Wittenberg suggests, "Kierkegaard's own publicness became for him a monumentally elaborate bad faith" (431).
7. For more on the question of presencing and the public see Alan Gross, "Presence as Argument in the Public Sphere" in *Rhetoric Society Quarterly* 35.2 (2005): 5–21.
8. Anonymous is discussed in more detail in chapter 7.
9. Strategic essentialism is a contextual strategy that allows for a part of one's identity or ideology to stand in for the whole.
10. The Pew Internet and American Life Project or the Center for the Digital Future's project (CDF) both are exemplary of this kind of scholarship.
11. For an example, see Lisa Gitelman's work (2003, 2006) on the relationship between new media and old media.
12. Slash fan fiction refers to those stories written by fans of a popular text (such as *Star Trek* or *Buffy the Vampire Slayer*) that pairs two characters in a romantic or sexual relationship. The "slash" refers to the punctuation mark found in many of the titles of these stories (e.g., Spock/Kirk, Buffy/Angel, Fred Flintstone/Barney Rubble). Slash fan fiction is often seen as a liberating form of fandom that removes the barriers imposed by the creators of the original work.
13. Her explanation for how she comes to use the term "community" comes when she invokes Henry Jenkins' (1992) argument that the very act of storytelling is "communal, wherein the sum of these minor alterations represents the story of a community in which each member has contributed to the corpus" (373).
14. Hebdige's famous study of punk subculture argues that "individual subcultures can be…integrated into the community, continuous with the values of that community, or extrapolated from it, defining themselves against the parent culture" (127).
15. See also Zittrain, Jonathan. *The Future of the Internet and How to Stop It*. New Haven, CT and London: Yale University Press, 2008. Print.

Critiquing New Media Discourse

To follow up our broad discussion of the connections between new media technology, the public sphere, and critical theory in the last chapter we now turn to a discussion of a particular political event—the 2010 U.S. midterm elections—in order to highlight some important considerations for studying political rhetoric in new media contexts. Specifically, we begin by explaining the political climate leading up to and during the election, emphasizing the role of new media. In the second half of the chapter, we focus on how a rhetorical approach to critiquing new media allows us to better understand some specific uses of new media technology in the midterms.

Overview of Online Activity During the 2010 Midterm Election Season

Shortly before President Obama took office in 2009, outgoing President George W. Bush invited three of his predecessors—George H. W. Bush, Bill Clinton, and Jimmy Carter—to his office for a chat. On that occasion, a photo of the presidents was taken and widely distributed to the press. One cartoon commentary on the image featured text balloons above each of the prior presidents' heads. The text in the balloon read, "I'm glad it's not me!" This was a nice commentary on the situation in which incoming President Obama was likely to find himself—the worst recession in decades, a collapsing economy, and the disintegration of the financial sector.

President Obama's early months in office were filled with challenges and controversy. As we noted in chapter 1, one of his first challenges was to respond to public outrage in the AIG bonus controversy that arose when the public learned that a sizable portion of the taxpayer-supported bailout funds provided to financial firms during the 2008 financial crisis was to be used to pay bonuses to the firms' executives. The Obama administration responded by honoring the contractual commitments to provide the bonuses while at the same time placing constraints going forward on executive compensation at the financial firms.

Troubles during Obama's first year in office continued unabated, however. First, a plan for economic recovery had to be developed and implemented. After broad consultation with stakeholders and economists, the Obama administration passed the largest social spending bill in history, directing $300 billion into health care and education spending, along with tens of billions of dollars into food stamps, housing aid, unemployment insurance, and child care. A number of other initiatives were undertaken and passed, often with difficulty because Republican members of Congress disapproved of the measures they contained (Froomkin). By June 2009, a Gallup Poll reported that the president's approval rating was 62% approve, 31% disapprove—a rather respectable outcome, given the many challenges yet to be dealt with. (Gallup)

Citing Nathan Newman's August 2010 blog on the Obama administration's accomplishments, blogger Michael Froomkin posted on his blog *Discourse.Net* an account of some of the early Obama administration's successes. These included passage of the aforementioned recovery plan, passage of the SCHIP bill that provided health care to millions of uninsured children, protections of land against oil and gas drilling, and other achievements. Froomkin concluded:

> This is the first recession ever where we have provided health care insurance for the unemployed, where unemployment insurance was expanded to cover a high percentage of the unemployed, and other aid to them was expanded in such a significant way. Notably, in December the *New York Times* found that 61% of the unemployed approved Obama's handling of his job.

After making these observations, he added that "you basically have to go back to FDR to find this level of social and economic legislation enacted in the middle of a recession" (Froomkin).

Despite the measures used to implement policies to help the unemployed and the poor, however, conditions worsened further during the summer months of

2010. In September of that year, the Census Bureau released a grim report related to the effects of the recession on the U.S. population. The number of Americans living in poverty had risen to a 51-year high in 2009. The national poverty rate of 14.3% was the highest since 1994. Unemployment had risen to 9.3%, and was at 9.6% shortly before the midterm elections (Pugh). President Obama responded by saying that the grim news indicated that much work remained to be done, but he indicated that the groundwork for recovery had been laid. However, by mid-autumn 2010, the beneficial effects of the measures that had been taken were not evident to voters. Many people had lost their health coverage—from 255 million in 2008 to 194.5 million, presumably due to the drop in the percentage of people who had private or job-based coverage (Pugh).

By mid-September 2010, the mood of the electorate was not good. One Associated Press poll found that voters disliked both the Democrats and the Republicans for different reasons. While 60% disapproved of the job the congressional Democrats were doing, 68% frowned on how the Republicans were performing. Evidently, the Republicans' efforts to block or slow down legislation were not being well received. The only good news for the Republicans was that the voters who disliked Democrats seemed ready to vote in greater numbers than those who disliked the Republicans (Fram).

The Opportunities and Challenges for both Republicans and Democrats in the 2010 Midterm Elections

To fully understand the complications in and importance of the 2010 midterms, it is useful to recognize the factors that were in play for each of the two parties as the midterms approached in October 2010. The Republicans had a number of advantages in their favor, but they also had challenges. First, they had a war chest of potential contributors, including the U.S. Chamber of Commerce, which had contributed $2,902,690 in campaign contributions by mid-September; the Crossroads Grassroots Policy Strategies group tied to Karl Rove that had contributed $4,885,120 during the same time frame; and the National Taxpayers Union, which had contributed $894,320. The total monetary resources available to support Republican candidates reached $10,932,600, as compared with the resources available for Democratic candidates that totaled only $1,267,910, a fraction of what was awarded to their competitors (Luo).

Spending gaps of this magnitude were made possible due partly to the January 2010 decision by the U.S. Supreme Court to deregulate spending by corporations and special interest groups seeking to contribute to political campaigns. Called the "Citizens United Decision," after the conservative nonprofit group that brought the action, this ruling was a free speech ruling that held that the government has no business regulating political speech. The dissenters on the Court responded that allowing corporate money to flood the political marketplace would corrupt democracy. In any case, the McCain-Feingold legislation that had put controls on corporate spending was negated by the Court. In his weekly radio address, President Obama subsequently remarked that, although his administration had taken many measures to reduce the influence of corporate and special interests on policy formation, the Court's decision had "handed a huge victory to special interests and their lobbyists—and a powerful blow to our efforts to rein in corporate influence" (*Huffington Post*, "Obama's Weekly Address").

As the election approached, E. J. Dionne Jr., syndicated columnist for the *Washington Post*, complained that in the midterm election, "Corporations and affluent individuals are pouring tens of millions of dollars into attack ads aimed almost exclusively at Democrats." The extent to which unfettered campaign spending by advocacy and special interest groups influenced the election results in 2010 may be difficult to gauge in retrospect, however, but in all likelihood, there was an impact on the voters of some kind, primarily because of negative campaign advertising.

An additional difficulty faced by the Democrats was related to a certain amount of antipathy about the election among voters. As noted in the Associated Press poll we discussed, people who disliked Democrats early in the campaign seemed ready to vote in greater numbers than those who disliked the Republican candidates. On the other hand, 37% of Republican voters responded to polls indicating that they were more inclined to vote for an independent candidate as compared to only 17% of Democrats (Rasmussen Reports).

Despite the advantages they enjoyed and the benefits afforded to them by campaign contributions, the Republicans nevertheless had their own challenges to deal with. Republicans running for House and Senate seats in the midterms faced substantial complications because of the differing views held by existing incumbent Republicans ("the establishment") on the one hand, and other groups that one commentator labeled "the purists"—Tea Party representatives and other disillusioned outsiders on the other (Shribman).An October 3, 2010, column in the *Pittsburgh Post-Gazette*,characterized the uneasiness of Republican "regulars" when a Zogby International poll revealed that among likely voters "the Tea Party rated higher than either established party" (Shribman).

Perhaps the public response was due to ambiguity about what the various factions stood for. Shribman explained that there was a lack of a consensus-based Republican Party plan or agenda early in the campaigns. He described the then-existing governing platform as "the usual mix of tax breaks for small business, spending freezes, and a ban on federal funding for abortion, plus repeal of

Obamacare." In regard to the public reaction to Republican policies at that juncture, it's worth keeping in mind the nature of public sentiment as expressed in the generic congressional ballot referred to earlier. The results of that poll indicated that "most voters were skeptical about the Republicans' new national pledge to America," and, as of early October, "the number of voters who favor repeal of the health care law had fallen to its lowest level since the bill was passed by Congress in late March 2010." Shribman's analysis concluded that, as of early October, "the Republican Party is in the sort of chaos the Democrats thought they had patented" due to an absence of coordination and coalescence on issues, priorities, and strategy.

The 2010 Election and New Strategies in New Media

As had been the case with other components of the 2010 midterm campaigns, Web-based political activity decreased in the run-up to the election compared to what had been seen during the prior presidential election. In 2008, much was made by onlookers both during and after the election of Barack Obama's ability to success-fully use the Web to both attract and mobilize young voters. Though some of the same online tactics continued into the 2010 campaign, the general apathy and outrage felt by the polis meant a mass departure from both voting booths and Web-based political engagement.

Changing voter attitudes also meant that the Web stopped being an impor-tant source of revenue during the 2010 midterms as it had been in 2008. Voter dis-interest, coupled with the aforementioned Supreme Court ruling on corporate campaign contributions, widespread economic turmoil, and the growth of populist movements meant that many Democrats and some Republicans had difficulty rais-ing funds compared to 2008. In 2008, Obama raised more than $745 million for his campaign, and congressional Democrats raised $779,519,527 compared to Republicans' amount of $638,447,282. In 2010, however, congressional Republicans raised $907,818,352, while the Democrats raised $756,731,306 (Spangler).

However, despite the decrease in Web activity compared to 2008, there were still several revelatory uses of new media during the midterm elections. And while all indications are that the Web was not as consequential in 2010 as it had been in 2008 (due in part to less interest among young voters, perhaps), new forms of online activity during the campaign might be best understood as a trial run for the 2012 election.

Arguably, the most significant technological development for the 2010 midterm elections was the expansion of new media technology used by campaigns beyond a candidate's Web site. Many candidates created iPhone applications, produced video advertisements exclusively for the Web, engaged in "cyber-squatting" techniques used to promote false information about opponents, engaged potential voters via social media sites such as Facebook, and ventured into other emerging areas of digital campaigning. These experiments met with mixed success.

iPhone Applications

If social networking was the campaign darling of the 2008 election (and to a lesser extent the 2004 election), the iPhone application became the next evolution in connecting voters to one another and the campaign in 2010. Some of the most prominent candidates, including Harry Reid (D) and Sharron Angle (R) in Nevada, Charlie Crist (D) in Florida, Michele Bachmann (R) in Minnesota, and Meg Whitman (R) in California, produced regularly updated applications (apps) available to download for free through Apple's iTunes store. In addition, the Democratic National Committee and several third parties published official iPhone apps, while unofficial apps supporting the Tea Party, Republican Party, and other various candidates and issues were uploaded to the iTunes Marketplace (iTunes—Everything You Need to Be Entertained).

The vast majority of these iPhone applications were miniaturized versions of the content available on the candidate's Web site, with several—such as Charlie Crist's—primarily featuring links that automatically redirected app users to his campaign site. The more innovative ones, however, used features such as location tracking and visual alerts to connect supporters to one another and to help them better organize and plan events, stay informed about what was going on in the campaign, and take stock of the work that needed to be done before election day. Other applications employed the technology offered by the iPhone by focusing on visual content. For example, Harry Reid's application allowed users to employ the iPhone's camera and microphone in order to take photos and short videos and upload them to be considered for publication on harryreid.com. Similarly, Florida Republican candidate for the U.S. Senate Marco Rubio's campaign application featured an extensive gallery of images and other media that could be viewed with Apple's media software. Almost every candidate's iPhone application had an option for users to donate, sign up to volunteer, or read the candidate's Twitter feed or Facebook status updates.

While some high-profile campaigns used iPhone applications, many more did not use the technology. In fact, an October 2010 search of the iPhone Application store for key terms like "campaign," "election," "senate," "office," "house," or "governor" yielded fewer than thirty results related to the 2010 midterm election and several from candidates who had already been defeated in earlier primaries. Of the applications available, a healthy percentage of them came from relatively unknown candidates who seemed to want to use the medium to gain attention. One such example was Republican Billy McCue, who published an application to support his run for lieutenant governor of Pennsylvania. McCue, who also uses his campaign application to promote his Bible Trivia iPhone app, followed the lead of many of the more established candidates using the iPhone App Store and created an application that largely featured content from his Web site.

In many ways, the iPhone applications used by campaigns in the 2010 midterms are reminiscent of the earliest campaign Web sites from the mid-1990s: they are reproducing an older format in a new medium. Many of the earliest candidate Web sites could be described as simply designed informational sites that were largely digital reproductions of the brochures and pamphlets handed out on the campaign trail. As candidates were still learning how to use the Web, they stuck with content that they knew to work in another medium (print). Through the use of these emergent mobile applications, candidates are repeating much of that earlier process by shoehorning their campaign Web sites into a mobile application. Though there are small pockets of technological innovation in some of the campaign applications, the vast majority are not yet taking full advantage of the medium.

Twitter and Other Social Media

Created in 2006, Twitter.com allows users to post messages of 140 characters in length that can then be read by followers of a user's account. From the start, the site grew in popularity, increasing its numbers slowly through 2007 and 2008 before becoming immensely popular starting in 2009 (McCarthy). Though some candidates used the site to promote their campaigns in the 2008 election, it was not a significant tool for campaigns until the 2010 midterms when almost all candidates had their own Twitter feed.[1] High-profile candidates such as Rand Paul, the Republican–Tea Party U.S. Senate candidate from Kentucky, "tweeted" his very intentions to run for office.[2] Candidates used Twitter to advertise and comment on their campaign events, weigh in on those news stories that were relevant to their platform or interests, and even share personal anecdotes. Even after the 2010 voting had ended, Twitter continued to make political headlines when several candidates released statements of victory or concession via Twitter.

Twitter feeds of most politicians are monitored by more traditional forms of media, and 140 characters is often all it takes for a story to materialize or a controversy to unfold. Early in the election, Indiana Republican candidate for U.S. House Marvin Scott fired his campaign manager Stan Solomon for antigay comments left in Solomon's Twitter feed such as "U should not allow queers around kids"

(Browning). In a post-midterm example, a Twitter feed by former Alaska governor Sarah Palin was the subject of a brief scandal a few days after the November election when Palin marked a "favorite" photo found in Ann Coulter's Twitter feed. The photo she marked featured a church in New York City with a sign that exclaimed, "The blood of Jesus against Obama History made 4 Nov 2008 a Taliban Muslim illegally elected president USA: Hussein" (Kolawole). Palin later unmarked the picture as a favorite, explaining that it was a mistake as she didn't know Twitter even allowed users to mark photos as such.

Despite the growth in Twitter usage, candidates continued to focus on other forms of social networking and social media that they had used previously into the 2010 campaign. Facebook continued to be a campaign staple and the best way to develop a digital following (Nielsen), with virtually any and every candidate having a Facebook page where they could share messages, images, and video in order to try to cultivate a following. Newcomer Foursquare, which amassed 50,000 users on election day (Scola, "Judging"), served to surpass some of the past success of a service like Meetup.org.

The actual voting impact of these social media sites is still indeterminate. We do know that a significant portion of social media usage by voters took place via cellular phones. A Pew report suggested that 26% of adults "used their cell phones to keep up with election news, warn friends about long lines at polling places, and even to make campaign contributions" (Sewell). In addition, the *New York Times* reported that a new technique known as "sentiment analysis" rose to prominence during the 2008 campaign, which uses software to track online discussion across social media and elsewhere to get real-time information on the electorate's mood:

> Because the technique passively monitors conversations, it can track which ideas develop organically, something that is unlikely to happen in traditional polling when respondents reply to specific questions. . . ."We're not necessarily seeking to replace—immediately, in 2012—the traditional mechanism. But it's got to have a seat at the table," said Michael Urban, who worked on several Republican campaigns." (Brustein)

If social media usage continues in subsequent campaigns, sentiment analysis may help us understand the connections between collecting digital followers, making certain kinds of postings, and voting results.

Cybersquatting

Not all those using new media in the 2010 campaigns were trying to capitalize on past successes or looking to create new ways of engaging voters; some campaigns found more nefarious uses of technology to take down the competition. One especially notable use in 2010 was political cybersquatting, the act of buying a domain name (Web address) that would be likely to attract visitors for a competitor. The goal of cybersquatting ranged from misinforming unsuspecting voters who visited the site, to blackmailing an opposing campaign into buying the domain, to simply taking away a potential resource of an opposing candidate.

CBS News reported on several of these sites from the 2010 midterms including bobmenendez.org, a site run by Sharron Angle's campaign to derail Harry Reid; joesestak.org, a site bought by Sestak's opponent Pat Toomey that features a Flash game meant to "Send Joe BACK to SCHOOL"; and other sites from less high-profile candidates, all of whom were using a legal tactic that, as Josh Bourne the president of the Coalition Against Domain Name Abuse (CADNA) put it, "for members of Congress, identity squatting can lead to misinformation, confusion among constituents and damage to their reputation" ("Identity Squatting Can Cost Members of Congress Their Reputation"). Other victims included Meg Whitman (DE), who had to settle out of court to acquire WhitmanFor Governor.com and MegWhitman2010.com, Brad Ellsworth (IN), and Trey Grayson (KY). CADNA reported, "Of the 100 senators and 435 representatives, 111 did not own any of the six domain names [related to the candidate's name] examined in the study and 185 owned only one. At the time of the study, only one member owned all six domain names."

There were other new media strategies utilized in the 2010 midterm campaigns, many of which had been seen in previous campaigns. Campaign Web sites continued to be important. Blogs by candidates and their support network featured prominently in e-campaigns, as did online message boards, meet-up planning sites, fundraising and volunteer portals, and any number of other Web-based tools seen in previous elections. Official flash-based video games were used to entertain and educate supporters while several unofficial ones, such as *Ed Martin is Hack-man* (Ed Martin Is Hackman), were designed to target opposing candidates. Campaigns increasingly released professionally created online video messages that went into much more detail than could be seen in a brief television spot.

Some Practical Considerations for the Rhetorical Study of New Media

Trying to determine the significance of this wide range of political uses of new media technologies poses something of a challenge to the rhetorical critic. How can we assess the wide range of activity found across these iPhone apps, social media sites, and regular campaign Web sites? What do we make of cybersquatting, flash games, or any other number of instances of digital political rhetoric found in the 2010 midterms? What components of particular messages are most salient?

This problem initially seems to be compounded by the rhetorical tradition. That is, the critical theory that comprises much of the history of rhetorical inquiry was designed for the study of speeches or the written word, and its application to new media technologies is not immediately apparent. Nonetheless, as we covered in the previous chapter, scholarship in those disciplines most concerned with the rhetorical tradition has increasingly addressed digital texts and contexts.

James Zappen's essay "Digital Rhetoric: Towards an Integrated Theory" engages many of the themes emerging from this rhetorically focused new media scholarship and provides us with a useful set of ideas from which to begin analyzing the kinds of new media phenomena seen in the 2010 midterms as well as in instances of digital rhetoric, more broadly.

Surveying existing scholarship, Zappen points to slippages among critics in the use of key terminology, in the application of ideas, and in divergent attempts to define what might count as digital rhetoric. He argues that any emergent theory of how new media functions rhetorically is little more than "an amalgam of more-or-less discrete components rather than a complete and integrated theory in its own right" (323). Furthermore, he suggests that those writing on digital rhetoric can be divided into three camps: those focusing on how persuasion has changed in online contexts (Welch; Warnick, *Critical Literacy*), those who focus on the construction of identity and community in cyberspace (Turkle); and those who are more interested in theorizing how certain aspects of digital technology itself might necessitate new models of rhetorical critique (Manovich; Gurak). He suggests that these theories might be combined ("integrated") to provide a more functional definition of "digital rhetoric" that would allow for rhetoricians to speak with instead of across one another. Each of these foci also serves as a useful jumping-off point for considering what it means to study political uses of new media from a rhetorical perspective.

Consideration 1: Rhetorical Persuasion in New Media

Since ancient Greece, rhetoric has been concerned with the study of how persuasion occurs. For the Sophists, Aristotle, Isocrates, and other early Greek rhetoricians, persuasion could be studied through the analysis of one's speeches and their comportment in the public sphere. Often, those observed by early rhetorical scholars were the important political and social figures of their day. By studying the attempts by powerful figures to persuade their audiences, rhetoricians gained an appreciation of how political change occurred. Many of their influential writings specifically addressed how pitch and tone, gesture and movement, personal character, and carefully crafted ideas could engage or repel an audience. Indeed, many of the concepts that are foundational to rhetorical theory and criticism such as ethos, logos, pathos, the canons of oratory, *techne*, *doxa*, and tropes can be traced back to the earliest recorded history of the discipline. A concern with the "available means of persuasion" is synonymous with rhetoric itself and recurs through the discipline's theoretical canon.

The first edition of this book was subtitled "Persuasion and Politics on the World Wide Web" because contemporary rhetorical analysts have that same need to understand how persuasive strategies form the foundations for political change. Today, studying speeches and public comportment may not necessarily be the best means of understanding this process. Since new media technologies function as a significant part of our political culture, candidates, voters, and critics must come to terms with how to make sense of persuasion in a digital medium.

Studying how persuasion works in digital contexts is both similar to and markedly different from studying persuasion in a speech, in a television advertisement, or in a courtroom. First, the Web employs a logic of referentiality and intertextuality where discourse is often characterized by fragmentary and disjointed statements and questions. In addition, Web-based discourse might not always share the commitment to rationality that we associate with most forms of argument or persuasion, and so applying traditional communication models like Toulmin's Model of Argumentation or the Elaboration Likelihood Model (Petty & Cacioppo) won't always yield productive results. Similarly, forms of rhetorical criticism such as narrative criticism or pentadic analysis that traditionally focus on more linear and self-contained discourses might not apply to the hyperspatial and hypertemporal nature of the Web without some adaptation.

The question of course, comes in *how* and *when* to adapt or combine these existing rhetorical methods and perspectives to the study of new media. Toward that end, we hope to demonstrate through subsequent chapters several ways of evaluating persuasion that take into account both the history of rhetorical inquiry and the ways in which digital contexts shape discourse. A brief look here at one example from the 2010 midterm will help foreshadow some of this discussion.

Example: Christine O'Donnell's Witchcraft Crisis

In the 1990s and early 2000s, Christine O'Donnell worked for several conservative groups, including her own Savior's Alliance for Lifting the Truth (SALT), as a lobbyist and spokesperson, appearing frequently in congressional offices and on television talk shows such as Bill Maher's *Politically Incorrect* to argue the validity of her positions on issues related to politics, sexuality, and religion. In 2010 O'Donnell ran on a family values platform as the Republican–Tea Party candidate for the U.S. Senate from Delaware. While she was running, Bill Maher showed a clip of O'Donnell appearing on his 1999 show saying, "I dabbled in witchcraft. I never joined a coven. I did…I hung around people who were doing these things. I'm not making this stuff up….One of my first dates with a witch was on a Satanic altar and I didn't know it" ("Christine O'Donnell Practiced Witchcraft"). The clip garnered a lot of attention, prompting the mainstream news media to pick up the story and O'Donnell to answer questions on the campaign trail from some of her confused supporters. The clip also went "viral," earning millions of hits on video sites like YouTube and spawning lively discussion, blog postings, and user-made response videos.

Eventually, O'Donnell's campaign released a formal TV commercial where O'Donnell refuted the claims by looking squarely into the camera throughout a commercial that features her in one long shot across a blue background. In the commercial she explained:

> I'm not a witch. I'm nothing you've heard. I'm you. None of us are perfect, but none of us can be happy with what we see all around us: politicians who think spending, trading favors and backroom deals are the ways to stay in office. I'll go to Washington and do what you'd do. I'm Christine O'Donnell and I approve this message. I'm you. ("Christine O'Donnell: I'm You")

As an attempt at persuasion and a refutation of a misleading story, the commercial is well presented and stated. It is basic. Many of the best remembered and most successful political advertisements in history have been simplistic, employed basic imagery, and voiced little commentary or elaboration (Johnson's *Daisy* ad ["LBJ Daisy Ad"], Bush's *Willie Horton* ad ["Willie Horton 1988 Attack Ad"], etc.). O'Donnell's most straightforward strategy in this ad is an attempt at Burkean identification through the repetition of the phrase "I'm you" and references to shared ideas and beliefs between O'Donnell and her voters (e.g., "none of us").

However, the exigency that the clip was responding to was not simply one of misinformation. The witchcraft narrative wasn't simply the result of a case of attacks made by her opponents to the voters in Delaware. The situation was much larger, and O'Donnell's ad fails to realize that she was not just addressing a local TV audience.

The ad should have been a response to a phenomenon that had largely taken place online, where a large audience of Web users had posted and reacted to a clip from a relatively low-rated opinion show (HBO is a premium channel) about a candidate from a relatively small state. The video response by the campaign failed to take into account that O'Donnell's audience of people who were interested in or involved with the witchcraft controversy extended well beyond the voters in her state or the select viewership of a particular show. By failing to recognize and address this larger, Web-using audience, O'Donnell's ad failed to persuade viewers that she was a worthy candidate.

Moreover, the ad probably did more to damage O'Donnell's campaign than to help it. The very simplicity that makes the ad effective as a tool for persuasion on television makes it ineffective for a Web climate rife with parody. Whereas the first witchcraft clip from 1999 caused a few video responses, a YouTube search reveals many more parodies of her "I'm not a witch" commercial.[3] For example, YouTube user britehorn posted a video featuring dolls of O'Donnell and Harry Potter characters against a blue background like the one used in the campaign advertisement. The doll of O'Donnell explains:

> I'm not a witch. But if I was going to be a witch, I'd be a good witch, like my friend Ginny Weasely from the Harry Potter films. Everyone likes Harry Potter. None of us are perfect, and especially not my friend Belatrix LaStrange who'd like to see you all dead. I'll go to Washington where I'll be pretty, smile a lot, and pose for the cameras every chance I get. I'm Christine O'Donnell and I approved this message that my media handlers told me to read. I'm Stupid. I'm you. ("Christine O'Donnell: 'I'm Not a Witch'")

Even more interesting, perhaps, and indicative of the quality of production that can be found on political parody videos, was the auto-tuned version of "I'm not a witch" uploaded by YouTube user schmoyo, which turns O'Donnell's ad into a musical number, using audio manipulation software to make her speech sound like a song. This video has more than 2.5 million views. Other videos included actual witches (e.g., Elvira) claiming not to be a witch in a similar style, users commenting on the commercial via Webcam, and other responses to the campaign's commercial. Collectively, these responses do more to denigrate O'Donnell than the original viral video she responded to did.

Consideration 2: The Rhetorical Construction of Identity

In the previous chapter we discussed how public sphere theory—especially counterpublic sphere theory—is concerned with how one's identity is shaped by participation in a public. Interest in rhetorically constituted subjectivity and its expression has marked much of contemporary rhetorical theory, to the extent that James Jasinski has suggested that there has been a "constitutive turn" in the field, with greater attention placed on how rhetorical practice "helps to produce or constitute a social world" (Jasinski in Parry-Giles and Hogan, 192).[4] That emphasis on identity can certainly be extended to any criticism interested in new media.

Processes of rhetorical identity construction are as varied and complicated in new media as they are anywhere else. The obstacles that a hypertextual context introduces for a theory of rhetorically constituted identity do not foreclose the possibility that identity formation can occur without the use of constitutive texts. In fact, a hypertextual landscape provides for an especially fluid and metonymic identity; digitality affords the possibility of abrupt change, erasure, and creation of identities new and old as situations and events necessitate. Sherry Turkle comments on this view of cyber-identity when she writes:

> The anonymity of [online games known as] MUDs gives people the chance to express multiple and often unexplored aspects of the self, to play with their identity and to try out new ones. MUDs make possible the creation of an identity so fluid and multiple that it strains the limits of the notion. Identity, after all, refers to the sameness between two qualities, in this case between a person and his or her persona. But in MUDs, one can be many. (241)

Here the definition of "identity" itself is called into question because the term conjures notions of fixity and stability, two features lacking from what has been observed in identities aligned with new media texts.

How, then, might a rhetor attempt to argue for or construct these particular and contingent identities outside of using constitutive discourses? The potential answer to this question is to be found in the distinction between content and form. Lev Manovich suggests that those processes of identification that we use to construct identity in interactive environments emphasize shifts in mental patterning that correspond to the interactive, hypertextual, mediated representational practices that denote digitality:

> The cultural technologies of an industrial society—cinema and fashion—asked us to identify with someone else's bodily image. Interactive media ask us to identify with someone else's mental structure. If the cinema viewer, male and female, lusted after and tried to emulate the body of the movie star, the computer user is asked to follow the mental trajectory of the new media designer. (61)

What Manovich strongly suggests about identity in this passage he indirectly argues many other places in his influential work: any theory of digital rhetoric will necessarily need to attend to that most striking feature of digitality—a shift in discursive form.

As discussed above, it was evidenced in the 2010 midterms that social-networking sites have become important centers of discourse in political campaigns. Communication occurs not just between a candidate and his or her audience but also among the members of the networking sites. Importantly, most sites offer a plentitude of tools that allow users to construct their virtual identity in the ways that allow us to observe that "mental structure" to which Manovich alludes.

Example: TeaPartyNation.com's Social Networking Site

One such site where users can construct a virtual identity is TeaPartyNation.com (TPN), a Web site that

> consists of a user-driven group of like-minded people who desire our God-given individual freedoms written out by the Founding Fathers. We believe in Limited Government, Free Speech, the 2nd Amendment, our Military, Secure Borders and our Country. (Tea Party Nation)

Much of the site's content is user-generated, and they boast a fairly active community on their social network (they had more than 36,000 members on the network as of January 2011) (Tea Party Nation, Members). The network itself runs on software created by Ning, a company that creates and sells social-networking technology catering to the needs of a particular Web site or group ("Create a Social Networking Site with Ning"). The TPN network features many features that have become standard on similar sites including settings for privacy, the ability to add photos and video, the ability to link your profile to other social-networking sites (such as Twitter), the ability to add friends, comment on people's digital wall, post your own status updates, and more.

One crucial distinction between TeaPartyNation.com and other, more popular social-networking sites is that TPN is a private social network that only admits members after a period of review. Whereas a site like Facebook, MySpace, or Twitter will allow new users to join very quickly after filling out the appropriate form fields, TPN social-network account hopefuls are required to submit their information and then await a decision. Presumably, that screening process includes checking into someone's political leanings, as they clearly state:

> Note to Prospective Liberal Trolls:[5] TPN does not tolerate liberal trolls. If your sole purpose is to join this site in order to disrupt the flow of constructive dialogue against liberalism, you will find your time here very short. You can and will be banned for being a liberal. If you wish to debate the virtues of liberalism (as though there were such a thing), there are many other sites on the Web who will tolerate you. TPN is not one of those sites. Tea Party Nation reserves the right to ban anyone for any reason we feel necessary to ensure the well being of the site and our members. (Tea Party Nation, Frequently Asked Questions)

This warning listed on the site's FAQ (Frequently Asked Questions) link is a good indicator as to what kinds of discourse take place on the social-networking component of the site. Otherwise, other than the political component and the close moderation, the rest of TeaPartyNation.com's social-networking site doesn't include anything especially novel. The site's features most closely mirror Facebook's, and how members of TPN use social networking to interact in a similar fashion as to what is done on Facebook, with a few interesting twists.

For example, since the Web site is a politically oriented one, users are invited to join their state or region's networking group so as to plan local meet-ups and share news stories with geographical relevance. In addition, many members take advantage of the site's blogging features to sound off on perceived problems. Users choosing the default settings for the site will receive several e-mails daily with links to these posts. For example, in the first week of 2011, the site sent out notices to members to read blog entries with the titles such as "The Death Screams of Howard Dean's Brain," "Taking Back the GOP in 2011," "Don't Steal, the Government Hates Competition," "Obama Doesn't Care," and "The People Strike Back!" Following the links in these e-mails brings users to the articles on the site and allows them to comment on specific entries with other users. Since these commenters also have their own pages set up on the social network, their responses to the blog entries link back to their own profiles so that other members can see their information.

The site is also interesting because one aspect of each person's identity—their political ideology—is generally the same as that of other users on the site. This requires users to differentiate themselves from one another in other ways, such as decorating their page with gifts from other members or sharing photos and videos of their families, pets, vacations, and so on. Strikingly, the site doesn't allow for much individualization beyond this—many of the form fields found on other social-networking sites that allow members to explain their interests, relationship status, hobbies, favorite entertainment, educational or career background, and so on are quite noticeably absent from TPN's social-networking site. Thus, the "networking" takes place almost entirely in ways which are tied to political ends, such as geography. The net result is that TPN users wishing to use social media to help establish an identity for themselves in an online space, to be that "new media designer" that Manovich describes, are left with few tools to do so.

Consideration 3: The Rhetoric of Technology

While analysis of persuasion and identity are two longstanding tropes of rhetorical theory and criticism, with the growth of new media technology scholars in the discipline have increasingly turned their attention to the importance of the medium itself in shaping how ideas are communicated. In and of itself, this focus on a medium is not a new idea in rhetorical criticism. Even the Greeks were interested in how the voice or the body played a role in shaping an audience's response to speeches, and rhetoricians have long considered film, television, radio, and other modern media technologies. John C. Adams argues that new media are an example of what Aristotle termed an "inartistic proof," the part of a speech that exists independently of a speaker's own ideas but can be creatively used by the speaker to enhance their speech. Moreover, the medium also serves as a context and a constraint on discourse, facilitating some kinds of communication while limiting others.

When confronting the role of technology in shaping both cultural change and temporal changes in rhetorical practice, critics often grapple with the question of technological determinism. On the one hand, a determinist view understands technology itself to be the most significant indicator and catalyst of social and cultural change, determining how rhetoric is crafted, disseminated, taken up, and so on. On the other hand, a relativist view of technology understands technological innovation as just one factor in ongoing cultural change and holds that technology is molded to fit the changing needs of society (rather than the other way around).

Dale Bertelsen's 1992 essay on how changes in political systems reflect changes in technology is illustrative of a more determinist view. Bertelsen's essay traces important historical distinctions between primary oral culture, which functioned as a basis for a participative and communally based democracy, secondary oral culture–literate culture, which functioned as a basis for an oligarchic society where citizens have indirect access to governance, and electronic culture, which he argues functions as a basis for a meritocracy wherein globalization makes expertise requisite for meaningful engagement in politics. The essay foregrounds technological change as a primary catalyst for shifts in political praxis, and Bertelsen suggests that

> to fully understand the relationship between media and social covenants, such as government, researchers should specify the technological and cultural systems in which those social covenants are considered. (332)

Likewise, John Jordan's 2003 essay addressing online shopping sites and the ways in which they use various Web-based technologies to shape users' view of their bodies is a similar example of scholarship that considers technology itself as a rhetorical force. On the 3D models used on the sites, he explains

> What makes this compelling is the way in which modeling technology generates this idealized self from the shopper's own input, thereby transferring responsibility for the image onto the shopper while simultaneously asking that the shopper desire the virtual model. (264)

In Jordan's essay, in Bertelsen's work, and in canonical media studies scholarship by thinkers like Marshall McLuhan and Neil Postman, a medium is more than just a context in which communication occurs, it is a constitutive feature of the discourse itself.

An example of a more relativist view of a technological influence can be seen in a recent essay by Dylan Wolfe, who explores how the relational and social elements found in viral video sharing do more to determine the significance of this kind of new media discourse than the medium itself.[6] He writes that understanding how the video circulates "requires considering what relationships are generated" (325) between the sites where the video is viewed, its users, and other contextual factors: "The most obvious of these user produced lines are connections between [the viral video] and new viewers" (328). It is important to note, like any technological relativist, Wolfe takes a more humanistic view of rhetoric, one that recognizes that "rhetorical contingency can only be addressed in each historical moment" (330).

This question of the technology's relationship to human agency is an important one that bears full consideration, as we will do in chapter 7. However, a brief look at one new media component of the 2010 midterm elections provides insight into the kinds of conundrums posed by this question.

Example: Foursquare and the Election

Howard Dean's enormous early success in the 2004 election season was attributed, in part, to his innovative uses of the Web to organize supporters and plan meetings and events. Since then, every election cycle has seen the Web used in new ways as a tool for getting voters energized; Meetup.com, Facebook.com, and even candidate-specific sites like My.BarackObama.com have all been used successfully at different moments in past campaigns to generate support. In the 2010 midterms, Foursquare became an important part of the election landscape.

Foursquare, a company that launched in 2009, has more than 5 million users and is one of the fastest-growing social media companies in the world, boasting more than 25,000 new users a day (Barbierri). Foursquare's popularity is due primarily to their mobile device applications, which according to their Web site,

> aims to encourage people to explore their neighborhoods and then reward people for doing so. We do this by combining our friend-finder and social city guide elements with game mechanics—our users earn points, win Mayorships and unlock badges for trying new places and revisiting old favorites. ("Foursquare")

Users of the service can post their location and invite others, check in when they have arrived at a location listed on the service, and, over several visits, become favorably associated with the places they visit most frequently by earning virtual badges of distinction. Specifically, Foursquare is an example of geosocial media, in that it uses GPS data to plot the coordinates of people who are linked together on a social network, making it possible for them to see where one another is via a software interface. Per the marketing Web site KnowThis.com, the technology also functions as advertising tool:

> The idea behind the integration of these two technologies rests with the ability of marketers to display ads and promotions to potential customers as they approach locations where a product can be purchased. Marketers see geo-targeted promotions as an excellent opportunity to stimulate impulse purchasing. For instance, knowing a customer is in a downtown shopping area at noon could be an ideal time to send a special lunch promotion for a nearby restaurant. (Christ)

Foursquare is available for iPhones, Android and BlackBerry devices, Palm devices, and a host of other platforms (Foursquare).

On election day 2010, Foursquare created a special badge for its users to indicate that they had checked in at a voting location. According to the company their "I Voted" campaign was both an attempt to generate turnout as well as to pilot a larger effort to be undertaken in 2012. On their Web site, they explained that "I Voted" would

> 1. Encourage civic participation through the distribution of the I Voted Foursquare badge for all Foursquare users who "shout" that they voted (variations count: vote, voting, voted) while at a designated polling location, 2. Increase transparency at polling locations by visualizing the time of day, check-in volume and gender of those checking in, [and] 3. Develop a replicatable & scalable system to use for the 2012 Presidential Election based on learnings from the data that is produced for the 2010 Midterm Elections. ("I Voted")

According to their visual data, which tracked check-ins at various geographic levels, more than 50,000 users checked in on election day, each earning their own badge.

To put this occurrence into focus given the discussion of the rhetoric of technology above, it is possible to read the significance of this event in different ways. From a technological determinist point of view, the technology has instigated new motivations for and experiences during voting. That is, the "lesson" of Foursquare's election day experiment is that geosocial media transformed how users think about voting and the benefits it entails (badges, recognition by friends on the network, registration as a data point, etc.). From a technological relativist view, these benefits are part of an ongoing shift in a wide variety of cultural practices toward individualization, game playing, narcissism, technological integration, and any number of other phenomena found outside of the election day experiment: Foursquare's efforts were created not as a way to change citizen's views of voting but to actualize existing beliefs about what voting should be.

Conclusion

In this chapter we have discussed how studying politics in new media contexts requires a careful consideration of the relationship between cultural and technological change, emphasizing how rhetorical theory provides the tools to do so. In the next chapter, we examine another feature of new media—interactivity—and discuss how rhetorical theory might also help us make sense of its function in political discourse.

Notes

1. Almost 90% of U.S. House candidates had a Twitter fee. (Nielsen).
2. The first high-profile candidate to announce his candidacy in an election via Twitter was San Francisco Mayor Gavin Newsom in 2008.
3. Not lost on many of these parodies was the fact that "I'm not a witch" is a line from the cult classic and oft-quoted film *Monty Python and the Holy Grail*.
4. "Constitutive Rhetoric" focuses on the ontological function of rhetoric, and has been defined by Maurice Charland as that discourse that calls subjects into being. Constitutive rhetorics "provide individuals with narratives to inhabit as subjects and motives to experience…they insert 'narratized' subjects as agents into the world" (143). For further discussion about constitutive rhetoric, see chapter 6.
5. A "troll" online is someone who engages in constant argument baiting, "flaming," and other contrarian Web practices.
6. Further discussion of this essay takes place in chapter 4.

Interactivity

Its Nature and Functions in Online Communication

In the early years of the Internet, one aspect of the online environment that was then regarded as a relatively "new" concept was online interactivity. It was so highly prized that some researchers in online communication labeled it as "the Golden Fleece of the Internet." Now, what does it mean to say such a thing? The metaphor seems quite apropos, for like the ram's golden fleece sought by Jason and the Argonauts, online interactivity is something that is highly valued, yet there is little consensus about exactly where it is located or what it is. Is it a feature of the media technology, the communication context, or the perception of users (Kiousis; McMillan)?

Media researchers have viewed online interactivity primarily as an attribute of technological functions of the medium such as hyperlinking, activating media downloads, filling in feedback forms, and playing online games (Stromer-Galley; McMillan). As Jennifer Stromer-Galley observed, this features-based approach emphasizes media effects and assumes that users are interacting with the medium "without ever directly communicating with another person" (118).

On the other hand, researchers in computer-mediated communication have focused on user-to-user interaction such as is found in e-mail, social networking sites, and blog responses. Sheizaf Rafaeli's view is that full interactivity occurs only when messages sustain reciprocal exchanges between communicators. That is, a person sends a message; a respondent replies in terms relevant to the topic initiated by the first person, and then that person responds to the preceding response in a relevant way. This has been labeled "third order dependency" (Kiousis 359) because the third and later messages in the sequence are related to and extend the topic of the original message. This perspective, then, views interactivity as an artifact of message sequencing and reciprocal communication in the context in which communication occurs.

A third perspective on online interactivity views it as an artifact of what users experience and perceive. Researchers holding this view are primarily interested in how users process communicative messages in online environments. The requisite criterion in this framework is *that users must actively attend and respond to messages in order for there to be interactivity.* John E. Newhagen noted that those who support the idea of interactivity as perceived by users would maintain that "at least one human has to be engaged in information processing in order for interactivity to take place in . . . 'the true now'" (396).

These three approaches to studying interactivity have been so highly contested that Erik P. Bucy has rightly concluded that "after nearly three decades of study and analysis, we scarcely know what interactivity *is*, let alone what it *does*, and have scant insight into the conditions in which interactive processes are likely to be consequential for members of a social system" (373).

At this point, readers of this chapter might be wondering what interactivity has to do with rhetoric. After all, in communication studies interactivity is most closely aligned with interpersonal communication. Interactivity is nevertheless a significant linchpin in the rhetorical appeal of online messages. Speculating on the reasons for its importance could involve concepts initially considered by rhetorical theorist Kenneth Burke. Burke believed that persuasion generally is aligned with identification between people. Identification is best promoted through division; that is, people come to identify with common interests by separating themselves from opposing groups and interests. Burke noted that "we are clearly in the region of rhetoric when considering the identifications whereby a specialized activity makes one a participant in some social or economic class [or, one might add, political party]. 'Belonging' in this sense is rhetorical" (*Rhetoric,* 28).

Burke also says that "the purest rhetorical pattern [is when] speaker and hearer [join] in partisan jokes made at the expense of another"(*Rhetoric,* 38). As will be seen in our examples of blog-based debate and deliberation in this chapter, online interactivity can play a key role in enabling proponents and opponents on an issue to refine their thinking on major political topics, identify major features at play in deliberation, and engage the interests of people who either share their views or oppose them. Thus, blog postings and political debates in other online forums are mobilized and enacted by means of interactivity and identification. Online interactivity, therefore, functions as a means of activating user responses and as a mode of address that can influence users and can itself be rhetorical in its effects. These actions bring to mind Burke's observation that "we must think of rhetoric not in terms of some one particular address, but as a general *body of identifications* that owe their convincingness much more to trivial repetition and dull daily reinforcement than to exceptional rhetorical skill" (*Rhetoric* 26; emphasis in original). On this view, attitudes are formed through such actions as signing petitions, donating to a campaign, activating media clips that ridicule the opposing candidate, and actively advocating for one's own candidate. Many of these actions are mobilized by means of interactivity and promote identification and, therefore, persuasion. Furthermore, rhetorical uses of style and modes of expression can be impersonal or can themselves can have an interactive quality about them. Thus, online interactivity as a means of activating user response and as a mode of address can influence users and can itself be rhetorical in its effects.

The purpose of this chapter is to show how online interactivity plays a role in deliberation about public policy by bringing users to identify with online advocates' views and positions. Before we examine how the process works, however, we will revisit the controversy that has surrounded the nature of interactivity and the forms of its use.

Interactivity: Sorting It Out

One focus of research on interactivity has been on interactivity as used on political campaign Web sites. This is because the Web's role in campaigning has grown in importance and extent since the first online campaign sites appeared in 1994 (Foot, Schneider, and Xenos). In each election cycle since then, the public's reliance on Internet-based political information has increased. In 2009, the Pew Internet and American Life Project reported that during the 2008 elections, some 74% of Internet users went online to get involved in the political process, which is the first time that Pew surveys have found that more than half of the voting-age population used the Internet to get involved in the political process during an election year. They also found that younger voters engaged heavily in political debate on social networking sites (A. Smith, "The Internet and Campaign 2010").

The importance of interactivity in online political communication has been emphasized by a number of researchers (Puopolo; Stromer-Galley and Foot; Endres and Warnick). In a primer for planners of online campaigns in 2002, the authors noted that "interactivity is one of the great distinguishing qualities of the Internet," and they advised their readers that to really engage, campaign sites must "take steps to leaven [their] Net operation's interactive features with interpersonal opportunities" (Institute for Politics, Democracy, and the Internet 25). To that end, they encouraged online campaigns to provide an offline method to reach the campaign, include polls seeking user opinions and post results, provide a sign-up for updates, maintain a secure online system for visitors to make campaign contributions, and provide online opportunities for supporters to volunteer. The primer concluded by saying that "when a campaign extends interactive features to the public, it signals a willingness to listen and learn from the people. That's a good image for the candidates to live up to" (25).

The practices advocated by these authors could be seen during the 2010 midterm elections when the Democratic National Committee developed the Web site Organizing for America, which included many of these features, including a sign-up where visitors could submit e-mail addresses and zip codes, maps of the United States showing which candidates were campaigning in a given state, and an interactive blog. This site was still being maintained after the 2010 midterm elections ended and was converted to a space where its content could be used for other purposes—primarily to campaign online for issues and measures backed by the Committee, such as repeal of the Don't Ask, Don't Tell policy (Democratic National Committee).

Those interested in studying the use of interactivity on political campaign sites (and other one-to-many venues) would therefore be well advised to consider the use of interactive mechanisms other than those using online person-to-person interactivity with third-order dependency. In this regard, Rafaeli's discussion of interactivity is once again helpful. He made a distinction between communication that he labeled "noninteractive" and interactive communication. In noninteractive exchanges, subsequent utterances in an exchange are not relevant to earlier messages in their nature or topic focus. Rafaeli contrasted this with "fully interactive" exchanges—message threads in which all subsequent messages were relevant to both the content and meaning of earlier messages. He also included a third category of "quasi interactive" or "reactive" messages in which a person sends a message to another person, who responds, and later messages refer to or cohere with the one preceding them. Classifying user responses to campaign attempts at interactivity as "reactive" is suitable, since most candidate campaign Web sites often opt for a quasi-interactive, one-to-many style of interactivity. This classification of three gradations of interactivity enables campaign site analysts to differentiate "fully interactive" from "quasi-interactive" or reactive responses to interactive features on political campaign sites. It is worth noting, too, that public blogs often tend to feature responses to an initial blog post that are not particularly relevant to the issue addressed and may, in fact, veer decidedly off topic. Rafaeli's distinctions can therefore be useful if there is interest in considering the extent to which blog discussions have some level of coherence and reciprocity in their ongoing interactions.

A second task, however, is to consider a form of on-site interactivity that has been identified by researchers interested in interactivity's role and effects in online political sites (Endres and Warnick; Warnick, Xenos, Endres & Gastil). This has been labeled "text-based interactivity," and lack of attention to it may have been due to new media researchers' interest in elements unique to the medium. Text-based interactivity has nonetheless been shown to play a role in users' reactions to online content involving political activity (Warnick et al.).

In the era of Web-based political campaigning, text-based interactivity refers to the presence of various stylistic devices, such as use of first-person and active versus passive voice; additional visual cues such as photographs of the candidate or supporters interacting with other people; and additional textual content on the site (Endres and Warnick). Such site elements function as rhetorical features of the site text that communicate a sense of engaging presence to site visitors. Campaign sites are purposefully designed to have a persuasive influence on their audience of users, and the use of expressive style, modes of self-presentation, and attentiveness to content have been shown to enhance users' reception of messages and recall of site content (Warnick et al.). It is for this reason that the Institute for Politics, Democracy, and the Internet urged campaigns to "extend a welcome greeting," "be concise," and include testimonials and endorsements from citizens not affiliated with the campaign (10).

As we consider the strategies used by online authors in blogs and other kinds of online discussion, the various forms of interactivity and the effects of its use in the progression of political discussion and debate will be clarified. Before proceeding to apply the concept to online interaction, however, it is necessary to consider the approaches taken by media researchers who have analyzed interactivity's workings.

A Useful Taxonomy of Interactivity

One of the prominent researchers in online interactivity, Sally J. McMillan, has traced the history and emergence of the interactivity concept as it applies to new media. She developed a typology of three forms of interactivity that have enabled analysts to identify communication patterns in online exchanges. These three forms are user-to-system, user-to-user, and user-to-document.

User-to-system interactivity is similar to the emphasis on the media technology as described at the beginning of this chapter. McMillan defined it as "computer-controlled interaction [that] assumes that the computer will 'present' information to learners who will respond to that information" (174). In such situations, the user activates a technical capacity of the system, and the system responds. User-to-system interactivity includes clicking on hyperlinks, customizing site features, and some gaming operations. Since this chapter will emphasize forms of interactivity insofar as they function as communication rather than as technologically enabled, user-to-system interactivity will play a minor role here.

User-to-user interactivity is communication that occurs between users and is aligned with the commuter-mediated communication orientation illustrated in Rafaeli's treatment of full interactivity. Examples on political sites include blogs with user comments and moderated discussions.

User-to-document interactivity in a new media context occurs when recipients of the message develop texts and information that change the content of the site text. In this form of interactivity, users become active co-creators of messages when they customize site content, vote in online polls, submit questions to be answered on the site, or post messages and photos that become part of the Web site text. In this sort of exchange, the Web site invites users to submit content; users send in materials; and then those materials are posted to the site for others to read. An even more frequent form of user-contributed cross-reference is when respondents on political blog posts include hyperlinks that can be further pursued by those readers who are interested in viewing the recommended content.

The case study analyses in this chapter will examine the uses of interactivity on political sites in a communication context and therefore will focus largely on user-to-user, user-to-document, and text-based interactivity. As noted earlier, the third of these forms of interactivity focuses on features of expression in the Web site text such as style, forms of expression, and use of visual images intended to enliven expression and engage user interests and response.

Background on Interactivity's Role in a Blog Controversy

To fully describe how blog-based public discussion unfolds, as well as the roles interactivity plays in this venue, we will consider a lively debate that ensued when a congressman appeared on CNN's *Parker Spitzer* show on 7 December 2010, to discuss the deal made between the Obama administration and Republicans on the extension of the Bush tax cuts. To enable readers to understand the issues that were at stake, it is necessary to provide some information about the tax-cut arrangement.

The initial tax-cut agreement announced by President Obama immediately became highly controversial. As reported by the *Washington Post* on 7 December

2010, the plan included extension of college tuition tax credit and other breaks for middle-class families that were due to expire by the end of 2010. It also revived the inheritance tax after a year-long lapse. The proposed plan was predicted to add more than $700 billion to the rising national debt, but it would also preserve administration tax breaks for families at all income levels for two years and extend emergency jobless benefits (which were about to expire) through 2011 (Bacon).

However, the part of the package that really disturbed progressive Democrats was President Obama's concession to the GOP to extend the Bush-era tax cuts that benefited the wealthiest 2% of U.S. households. President Obama had campaigned on a promise to repeal the tax cuts for the rich, and many of his former supporters were very angry about his "caving in" on this issue.

During his CNN interview, the title of which was "Anthony Weiner Asks President Obama to Quit Punting on Third Down," the congressman supported the president while explaining his concerns and reservations about Obama's tactics and his emphasis on bipartisan legislation (and bipartisanship between the two parties at that point seemed to be dysfunctional) (Video Café).

To understand public blogs in context, it's useful to know that they operate as an expressive genre of communication that begins with an initiating post by the blog author (or authors if it is a corporate blog). In the case of this interview, two CNN newsmen sought out his views about Obama's decision and challenged him on some of his online posts. The video and transcribed text of what he said were posted to the site, and below the posted text there was space provided for followers of the blog to state their views on the issues discussed.

In his responses to the interviewers' questions, the congressman was quite frank in his assessments of how the president had handled the development of the tax-cut proposal. The metaphor of "punting on third down" held sway during the lively and informative blog discussion that followed the pundit's televised analysis.

He noted that the president's claims and promises made when he was campaigning for president were not honored in the concessions he made on the tax cuts. He wondered why Obama did not "move the meter on these things" (i.e., his campaign promises), which included a pledge to end Bush-era tax cuts that benefit the rich.

The congressman expressed the view that the president should have taken a harder stance. He also noted that during the four weeks since the midterm elections, the president had not given a speech to the nation and had not stated his principles and intentions regarding the repeal of the "don't ask, don't tell" policy and fiscal matters affecting the public.

He described the president as being "beaten like a rented mule" by Republicans who seemingly did not buy into bipartisanship.

He also called for more leadership from the president. He noted that the president seemed to believe that "bipartisanship is an ends (*sic*) rather than a means." Both the interviewers and their guest agreed that President Obama seemed unwilling to put up the fight and resistance that would eventuate in some kind of acceptable compromise. The congressman also noted that the Democrats had accepted forty Republican amendments on the health care bill and wound up "getting zero votes back in favor of it."

These criticisms and assessments, as aired in the interview, brought to light gaps in the administration's resolve to overcome GOP resistance to proposed legislation over time.

Interactivity in the Subsequent Blog-Based Discussion of Weiner's Comments

The online dialogues that were sparked by this interview with CNN's interrogators were revealing in that they exposed the motivations and reservations of advocates for and critics of the Obama administration's tax-cut proposal. Arguments for and against the legislation were aired as the theme of the "quick kick play" (in football), and "punting on third down" played out.

For example, the first entry in the blog sequence by commenter 1 asserted the following statement about the president: "Face it. He's a wimp." This was quickly answered by commenter 2 who reminded readers that "one does not become the first black president of the USA by being a wimp. And one does not get to defeat the Clinton political machinery in the primaries by being naïve. [Obama] is just not a progressive. People need to grasp that already. He was pretty tough when he wanted funding extensions for the [Afghan] war, wasn't he?"

This response was representative of commenter 2's role as apologist for and defender of the president's actions as the exchanges on the blog progressed.

The next opponent of the tax-cut initiative and Obama's approval of it was commenter 3, who engaged in a rant: "Can't Obama see that the GOP is just setting…a trap? Cutting the payroll tax is the first step in eventually defunding Social Security entirely. The tax cuts for two years [in exchange for] thirteen months of unemployment. Is this guy stupid or what? . . . I've had it with this guy. He has no moxie at all. He rolls over at every opportunity."

Commenter 3 found a supporter when commenter 4 asserted that the president was "just a republican't." The blogger asserted that "there used to be a "D" somewhere around his name but it looks like that morphed into an 'R.'" It was beginning to appear that the more liberal and progressive contributors to the blog viewed President Obama as a conservative in disguise.

However, commenter 5 slyly asked "How come the GOP didn't 'cave' on unemployment?—OH, THEY DID!," thus implying that there was a quid pro quo embedded in the proposed legislation—extension of unemployment benefits that otherwise would expire for 2 million Americans at the beginning of January 2011 (Aguiluz).

At this point, a new theme (still dealing off the football meme previously introduced) was entered into the discussion by commenter 6. This is the idea of the "quick kick play" where the initiator of an idea puts opponents into a situation where they must commit to an action on short notice. Commenter 6 observed that "the House and Senate have the ball in their court now. If they think [the tax cut proposal] is a bad deal, vote it down. We will get to see who the real cowards are."

Commenter 7 picks up on this theme with commentary: "'The quick kick' was extremely effective on my old HS team for two reasons: 1) The other team wasn't expecting it. 2) Our offense sucked hard."

He concluded that "I guess BO [Obama] is basically admitting that the Dems' offense is um, very weak."

At this point, commenter 8 deflects attention away from strategy to complain about the President's choices of advisors—Rahm Emanuel as White House chief of staff and senior advisor to then President Clinton whom he viewed as a "reactionary social type." No one responded to this post.

Another critic, commenter 9, inserted a theme that had already been played out on the site. He maintained that "Obama isn't punting on the 3rd down, he's punting on the first."

An Obama apologist, commenter 10, then noted that Obama's compromise was consistent with his 2008 campaign message of changing the way that Washington works and doing what's right over what is popular. He concluded by saying, "The question is, will it prove disastrous for him in 2012?"

Commenter 11 then expressed concern about changes in the federal estate tax that were part of the proposed legislation, noting that extension of approval for continued unemployment benefits came at a very high price.

Commenter 12 then reiterated a concern that he had expressed earlier: "THE DEFICIT! THE DEFICIT! Entitlements must end!"

Commenter 13 then introduced a theme that will bring the discussion to a close:

> The trouble is—It's fourth down. Unemployment insurance benefits are running out right now and the Senate Democrats have failed to even get a vote on extending them. If the tax breaks expire without an extension of unemployment insurance benefits, there will never be a vote on an extension. The President had no choice but to make a deal with the devil. People will begin losing their homes RIGHT NOW. The Senate Democrats gave up all the leverage they had by waiting until after the election to even

begin considering taxes and unemployment. The President proposed a game plan. The Democrats in the House did their part; the Democrats in the Senate sat on the sidelines.

Commenter 14 immediately responds:

> Yes! Yes! Yes! Why didn't the majority party in the Senate take care of business months ago when they had the chance? The people who actually do the voting dropped the ball (It really is like a big football game). The President was not forced by the minority party to propose these terrible compromises. He was forced into it by the ineptness of his own party.

These exchanges in the blog thread nicely illustrate the need for and benefits of online interactivity. Participants in these discussions are clearly interested in specific political issues. As an aggregate, many of them seem well informed. Unlike some less functional blogs, the contributors to this discussion largely (although not exclusively) stayed on topic. Weiner's interview served to introduce a frame and implied a problem for discussion: Was the president "caving in" at the last minute, sacrificing principles he'd campaigned on, and making bad deals and concessions? Or was he implementing a compromise that would move the process forward while the existing Democratic office holders were still in place? Such a move would be more viable at the time he proposed it than later on after the newly elected Republican cohort arrived in the House and the Senate.

The group's emphasis on strategy, instigated by the congressman's "punting on third down" metaphor, served to constrain the focus of the blog discussion and enabled informed deliberation among participants as the thread developed. Their reciprocal exchanges and acknowledgments of the ideas that were introduced illustrate the ways that informed and reciprocal interactivity among knowledgeable people can deepen understanding, provide information, extend corporate thought processes, and clarify the issues at stake.

Tax Cut Legislation Post script

On 17 December 2010, it was announced that the House had passed President Obama's landmark unemployment extension legislation. The projected expense of the measure was estimated to be $858 billion, but nevertheless, it had enough support to pass the House 277–148. The plan, negotiated by President Obama and Senate leaders, extended current tax rates indefinitely for most earners and for two years for couples making $250,000 or more per year while also extending long-term unemployment benefits for another thirteen months. The vote earlier in the week in the Senate had been 81–19 in favor.

Democrats acknowledged that the payroll tax cut would drain Social Security funds, but they also were especially irked at the estate tax provisions. At the time of passage, the impact of the legislation on future fiscal outcomes remained to be seen.

Conclusion

In the years since the 2004 presidential election, the forms of interactivity in online political campaigning and commentary have changed from the use of comparatively static features such as online polls and candidate photo galleries and credentials to features designed to involve users in collaborative deliberation about political issues and events. These include the use of interactive blogs and social-networking sites that address political issues. Furthermore, when discussion and disclosures of campaign-related developments are made known to the public via public blogs, media outlets can broadcast these disclosures, and their readers benefit by becoming knowledgeable about what is going on behind the scenes and in the halls of Congress. Therefore, not only do interactivity and online discussion facilitate communication, they also enhance the potential for developing a more informed and attentive electorate.

Insofar as candidate Web sites such as Organizing for America can engage users, mobilize their constituencies, focus users' attention on vital issues relevant to the campaign, and keep them informed on progress related to their goals, the agenda of political advocates who sustain interest in their issues and concerns will have some impact.

As the Organizing for America Web site reminded its readers on 24 December 2010, the successes that the Obama administration achieved late in its first term were enabled through consistent and sustained advocacy in behalf of Don't Ask, Don't Tell Repeal; passage of credit card reform legislation, student loan reform, and other measures that Obama's 2008 campaign base had viewed as significant. To some extent, the necessary attention to these signal issues late in the congressional session kept lawmakers focused on the issues that otherwise might have been deflected in the final days of congressional action in 2010.

4

Circulation and Rhetorical Uptake

Viral Video and Internet Memes

One of the most popular videos ever published to the Internet is a fifty-second clip of an orange cat wearing a blue shirt and playing a keyboard. In the video, the cat's arms and body are being manipulated by an individual outside of the frame, and the cat's expressions during the brief song give the impression that the cat is "feeling" the soulfulness of his performance in the best tradition of Stevie Wonder or Elton John. The video is an amusing home movie, the kind of thing that was frequently seen on episodes of *America's Funniest Home Videos* when that series was popular in the early to mid-1990s.

As of this writing, that video has been viewed almost 12 million times on YouTube, and it has spawned numerous parody clips (including one aired on Comedy Central's *Tosh.0* featuring Kato Kaelin in the role of the cat), been featured on clothing and merchandise, and become a symbol for a phenomenon known as "viral video." Like Christine O'Donnell's "I am not a Witch" video mentioned in chapter 2, the keyboard cat video struck a nerve with online audiences in such a way as to cause the video to attain a meteoric rise in popularity, garnering many hits in a short period of time.

This chapter investigates these videos in order to shed light on what makes them connect with audiences as they do by providing an overview of viral video, explaining a case study, and offering discussion on how to understand their significance in the broader purview of digital rhetoric.

An Overview of Viral Video

For the purpose of this discussion, let's define viral videos as those that meet several basic criteria:

1. Viral videos receive a large number of views, usually in a relatively short period of time.

This can be assessed by considering two primary factors—the date a video was uploaded and the number of viewings the video has had. On sites like YouTube and Vimeo, both pieces of information can usually be found on the same page where a user would play the video. On other sites, such as Google Video, only an approximate date of posting is listed, with no statistical data provided. From studying sites that do list data, it seems that most viral videos (such as those listed in *Time's* "YouTube's 50 Best Videos") have received several million views at minimum, though videos that receive a high number of hits in a short period (e.g., tens or hundreds of thousands in one week), may also indicate that a video has become a viral video.[1] Another useful method for tracking a video's viral quality is offered by the Web site Mememachine, which tracks how often videos are shared by accumulating data from Facebook, Twitter, Blogger, and user comments on video-hosting sites.[2] For example, according to the site's data on 2 January 2010, a video of a school performance by preteen Greyson Chance singing Lady Gaga's song "Paparazzi" had generated 516,920 of what the site calls "shares," making it the top viral video for 2010.[3] It is worth noting that viral videos do not necessarily always "go viral" immediately upon being uploaded, as sometimes years will pass between the time a video is initially posted and when it attains popularity. This phenomenon can occasionally be seen on Web sites like Digg or Reddit, which collect user-submitted Web links that are then ranked in popularity by the site's users.

2. Viral videos generate a significant number of responses.

Statistically, this measure is a little bit harder to assess, but it is probably more significant for the rhetorical critic interested in studying viral video. What separates a viral video from other popular videos isn't simply the number of views but also the ways in which the video is taken up in both traditional and new media outlets. Viral videos often generate a significant amount of blog postings, response and parody videos, and re-airings on television news and comedy programs. For example, C-SPAN's YouTube video of Barack Obama's 2008 inauguration speech has garnered more than 4 million hits, but the video itself hasn't spawned near the amount of parodies, blog posts, and activity on social media–sharing sites as did the video "Hamster on a Piano (Eating Popcorn)" from the same year, even though the hamster video had fewer total views than the inauguration. A search on YouTube for "Hamster on a Piano" yields more than 400 videos that are repostings, homage, parodies, remixes, or other engagements with the original video. "Hamster on a Piano (Eating Popcorn)" has a Web site affiliated with the video where users can watch videos of hamsters eating popcorn in other locations, buy t-shirts and merchandise with the title of the video, and become Facebook friends with those involved with the video. In addition, "Hamster on a Piano (Eating Popcorn)" made *Time Magazine*'s list of Best Viral Videos of 2008, has been made into ring tone for cell phones, was discussed briefly and aired on MSNBC's *Rachel Maddow Show*, and covered in many blog postings across the Web. Even several years after the video was launched, one can still find "Hamster" t-shirts and merchandise for sale across the Web.

3. Viral videos rely heavily on pathos and novelty.

"Hamster on a Piano (Eating Popcorn)" is similar to another popular viral video produced by user ParryGripp featuring a musical montage of hamsters, mice, rabbits, and other small creatures eating food titled "Nom Nom Nom Nom Nom Nom Nom." This video, which has received more than 11 million hits in two years, is primarily remarkable for how "cute" the animals are and how apropos the music accompanying the video (with a refrain of "nom nom nom") is, given the subject matter. The fact that both videos have attained "viral" status is not a coincidence. A quick survey of any list of "greatest viral videos of all time" reveals that most rely on strong pathos elements such as humor and music, are relatively short (one to two minutes in length is common, almost all are under five minutes), and tend to each be different from other videos that have gone viral previously. In other words, though some successful viral videos utilize tried and true tropes of whatever respective genre applies in order to generate favorable emotional responses by audiences, the majority find resonance through the use of novelty. It is this novelty that plays an important role in facilitating peer-to-peer sharing and other forms of circulation across the Web.

Viral Video and Rhetorical Theory

While these three basic criteria (popularity, response, and novelty) help us understand what marks viral videos as distinct from other videos found on the Web, it is worth remembering that a YouTube video that has received 100 million views is just as enabled and constrained by the medium in which it appears as a video that has received one viewing. That is, if we put aside context and uptake, studying video on the Web shares much in common with studying video anywhere else we might find it. The wealth of existing scholarship on visual rhetoric (specifically the rhetoric of film) is quite useful when approaching videos to assess their aesthetic or narrative qualities, and though many Web videos are user-created or "amateur" video, that does not mean that they are somehow unique to new media.[4]

Some interesting scholarship specific to online video has already been done by rhetorical scholars, much of it indicating how some of the technological character-istics of new media might promote a different understanding of the significance of concepts like interaction and circulation. For example, Kephart and Rafferty's analysis of the "Yes We Can" campaign in the 2008 election and the resulting Will.i.am video on YouTube (which garnered widespread attention during the campaign and is an example of a political viral video) posited that the video func-tioned to perpetuate the "central trope" in the 2008 campaign:

> The 'Yes We Can' video is both intertextual and hyper-textual. The trope travels rhi-zomatically from auditorium to news channel to Internet and back into itself on tele-vision, in classrooms, on social networking sites, and every site imaginable. (17)

The concept of "rhizomatic travel" is a reference to work by Guy Deleuze and Felix Guattari that suggests that discourses of change travel or circulate much like a rhi-zome in nature—horizontally, with many points of connection and departure. Kephart and Rafferty explained that "a rhizomatic understanding of rhetoric is a useful lens" because it is well suited for the analysis of "rhetorical tropes in the con-text of a hyper-mediated political campaign" (7) and that the video proved to be a device that "establishes consubstantiality" (15) between various audiences and Obama.

The idea that viral videos might best be understood as video rhizomes is also the central thesis in Wolfe's essay on the viral video series *The Meatrix*, a collection of shorts that parody the *Matrix* films by using animated barnyard animals to warn about the dangers of factory farming. Arguing that the viral metaphor is flawed by "mechanistic thinking" (319), Wolfe suggests that the rhizome better captures the logic of activist videos that garner large followings. He explains:

> The so-called viral video is neither self-reproducing nor autonomous. The spread of both biological and computer viruses are involuntary to the host. New media texts, how-ever, spread not as an infection but through deliberate activity....Put simply, audience members are not at the whim of an autonomous infection, but, conversely, make indi-vidual choices regarding dissemination. (320)

In some comments that mirror chapter 2's discussion of critical disagreement over technological determinism, Wolfe even ventures that a "viral" view of video is deterministic, whereas a rhizomatic view emphasizes the relational, human component of these videos:

> In contrast to the mechanistic view of technological determinism, with predatory viral videos autonomously self-reproducing from an infected host, a relational view allows for understanding rhetorical function alongside technological characteristics. *The Meatrix* viewed as an assemblage focuses our attention on the connection between the text as a situated argument, its context as an emergent technological form, and the way it is experienced by viewers. (321)

Instead of offering a critique that focuses on the content of the video itself, Wolfe uses rhetorical criticism as a tool to trace the "lines" of relationships between instantiations of the video, responses to the video, and other aspects of a video's circulation.

This emphasis on uptake, shared by both Kephart and Rafferty and Wolfe, is reflective of the kind of rhetorical situation described by Barbara Biesecker (1989), one that emphasizes the contingent and subjective nature of discursive events. To study uptake is to move from studying the features and nuances of discourse as it occurs in an event to studying the effects and uses of that discourse in new contexts. Studying videos from the perspective of uptake is not an attempt to measure "effect" from the perspective of "intent" (e.g., if a video succeeded or failed), but from the perspective of citation. The critic asks: What is the continued usage of a discourse? What is its "citational legacy?"[5]

This perspective on how to apply rhetorical theory to the study of new media is one that is indebted to postmodern deconstructionist philosophy, and it is well suited to viral video for a number of reasons. For one, as Roderick Hart explains, from a deconstructionist point of view "all messages are intertwined" (317), and thus "we cannot escape intertextuality...subtexts affect not only how we listen and read but also how we are prepared to listen and read" (318). As is often the case with viral video, this intertextuality is either explicit in the video itself or can be found in comments and other text accompanying the video's circulation. That is, the videos may combine video and sound in novel ways, make allusions to other video (in parody, for example), or be contextualized by e-mails, blog posts, or comments surrounding the video frame. The analysis of viral video, then, is not simply a study of the video in and of itself but of everything surrounding it. It is this surrounding discursive context which gives evidence of a video's viral status. Aaron Hess points to the potential significance of the surrounding discourse of online videos when he writes of YouTube members who "utilize parody and the edge of irony as a strategy of resis-

[handwritten marginal note: "You tube God smoke 2008 campaign"]

tance that unpacks original messages through an intertextual negotiation of the original and the parodic" (481). Hess is referencing online activity surrounding a set of government-produced antidrug ads on YouTube; he eventually concludes that the majority of the accompanying comments, reply videos, and other surrounding discourse does much to undermine the potential of video sites to act as place of political deliberation. In the next section we will look at an example of viral video that did have political influence and that reveals some of the potential for the medium.

Case Study: Lady Gaga's "Don't Ask Don't Tell" Campaign

Pop singer Lady Gaga had the top-selling album in the world in 2010, moving over 6 million copies of her *Fame Monster*. The album's title aptly describes her success during the year, as she was a frequent guest on talk shows and award shows, released multiple hit singles and music videos, and was nominated for consideration as one of *Time Magazine's* people of the year. As *Time's* Web site explained:

> If you like dance and pop, the music is great—well-produced and delightfully contagious. But the spectacle that is Lady Gaga is not really about the music, even though she did win two Grammys this year. It's not even about the outfits, including the crazy glam-rock bodices and odd headgear. Rather, Stefani Joanne Germanotta has become famous by being obsessed with fame....It's performance art, and at least for now, everyone is loving the performance. ("Full List—Who Will Be TIME's 2010 Person of the Year?")

Gaga's fame has certainly extended to the Web, as Google ranked her in the top 10 rising searches internationally in 2010 (for the categories of both "Entertainment" and "People"). It is no surprise, then, that Lady Gaga's online music videos have also been successful. As of January 2011, Lady Gaga's official YouTube channel boasts several videos with hundreds of millions of views ("Bad Romance" is the leader, with more than 300 million views). Especially interesting, though, is that of her videos first uploaded in 2010, the one with the most views is not a music video but a video titled "A Message from Lady Gaga to the Senate."

The message is a plea from Lady Gaga to the Senate to repeal the Don't Ask Don't Tell law that made it illegal for gay service members to serve openly. In the black and white video, Lady Gaga appears in a suit and tie in front of an American flag and begins by addressing "fellow Americans" and several senators who have either proposed the Don't Ask Don't Tell (DADT) repeal or who are on record for having spoken against the legislation. In the video, she says:

I am here to be a voice not of the generation of the senators who are voting, but for the youth of this country, the generation that is affected by this law and whose children will be affected. We are not asking you to agree with or approve the moral implications of homosexuality; we're asking you to do your job, to protect the constitution.

In the last several minutes of the video Lady Gaga places calls to New York senators Chuck Schumer and Kirsten Gillibrand, modeling the actions she wants the people watching the video to take (she doesn't get through to either directly though she leaves a message). The video is just a single continuous shot, without music or any other hints as to why Lady Gaga is a popular figure.

This video meets the requirements set out above for defining viral video. First, it received a large number of views in a relatively short period of time (more than 1.5 million in the first week) (Baumann and Corn). The black and white video was posted around the same time that another clip of Lady Gaga speaking at a rally in Maine about DADT was garnering attention on the Web; collectively the videos were viewed on YouTube more than 3 million times in 2010 and were subsequently picked up by other video-hosting sites. A quick survey of the Web in January 2011 shows that there are videos of Lady Gaga speaking about Don't Ask Don't Tell on video hosts vimeo.com, go.com, vodpod.com, mefeedia.com, blip.tv, metacafe.com, veoh.com, and elsewhere. Some of these hosted the video directed to the Senate, others featured the Maine rally, and still others hosted various media interviews Lady Gaga did with Larry King and others regarding the topic. Collectively, these videos suggest that Lady Gaga's presence on the Web as an advocate for a repeal of DADT from September 2010 on was pervasive.

Second, the video garnered the attention of other media outlets and spawned many reply videos by other YouTube users. Snippets of the video played widely on mainstream television news stations, Gaga's plea and some related Twitter activity between the singer and Harry Reid garnered reports and editorials from newspapers and online news sources, and at least one outlet even followed up on the story with the Pentagon (Lawrence). As *Huffington Post* editorialist Lynn Parramore put it,

> While members of Congress were suffering historical amnesia, pop singer Lady Gaga— dubbed a "sexual radical" by antigay activists—released a video urging senators and fellow Americans to push for repeal...Sen. Lindsey Graham (R., S.C.) heard it, but expressed his disdain: "Whether Lady Gaga likes it or not is not of great concern to me" because she's not in the military. The Senator's understanding of the issue of closeted gays in the armed forces aside, he is, undisputably, a politician. And that, alas, would be the American group last to get it on Don't Ask, Don't Tell.

In addition to the commentary and coverage from the mainstream press suggesting the video's viral character, a large number of response videos by other YouTube users also helped to highlight the reach of Gaga's message to the Senate. Some of these videos can be classified as "fan responses" wherein users expressed their understanding and appreciation for Gaga's video and pledged their support to help the cause. For example, students from the University of Colorado named Ellie and Lauren submitted a video to voteagain2010.com titled "Vote Again in 2010: Do it for Gaga" that featured clips from Lady Gaga's Senate video and other appearances talking about Don't Ask Don't Tell. Another common response by users was to mirror Gaga's action of calling their senator on camera, many even going so far as to reproduce aspects of Gaga's video (the flag, the lack of color, etc.). A video by user Brendiz16 titled "Brenda's Message to the Senate" is indicative of these responses. Perhaps the most interesting responses were those that parodied Gaga's message for a variety of purposes. The first result of a search on YouTube for "Gaga Senate Response" is a video titled "Dont ask dont tell Repealed DADT, KKK Response, Lady Gaga, News, Video," which, as the title suggests, is a response to Gaga's video by someone claiming to be from the Ku Klux Klan. The video parodies the original closely, with the hooded speaker in suit and tie placed in front of a similar flag with the video shot in black and white.[6] Other parodic examples include videos that openly disagree with the singer, bizarrely animated videos using the audio from the original, and a British man upset with Gaga's stance. Though not as widely taken up as some other aforementioned viral videos, it seems that Gaga's video appealing to the Senate did indeed garner the attention for the issue that she hoped it might.

Third, the video can be defined as a viral video in part because of its novelty. That is, it is unusual for the fact that it is a video made by Lady Gaga that doesn't feature fashion, music, or any of the other areas of interest that have made her a celebrity. While the concept of celebrities addressing political topics is not itself novel, the level of Gaga's popularity at the time of the video's creation undoubtedly added to its novel appeal. The form of address—direct comments to specific senators and a recorded phone call—also stands out from those videos in which celebrities discuss causes with audiences more generally, urge them to vote, or otherwise raise consciousness. Finally, the video's use of sharply contrasting black and white elements is a further departure from the flashy, colorful approach seen in most of Gaga's work. For these reasons the video stands out from other videos that tackle the issue of DADT, including those with celebrities.

"A Message from Lady Gaga to the Senate" functions as a useful example of how viral videos might have political importance, as it seems evident from the responses, views, and coverage that the video was seen by many of Gaga's fans as well as some of the general public. While her video wasn't a major cause for the repeal of DADT, it served a small role in gaining further public attention for a controversial legislative vote. On the other hand, it is also fair to say that, like other popular videos that address politics in some fashion (Will.i.am's "We are the Ones," Obama's Inauguration Speech, etc.), the total viewership is significantly less than those videos that feature cute hamsters, humiliating moments, or popular music. From a cynical point of view, politically relevant viral video faces an uphill battle in reaching an audience in a context that shares more commonalities with an episode of *America's Funniest Home Videos* or MTV than it does with C-SPAN or political talk shows. In the next section, we'll discuss why that might be.

Discussion: Circulation, Memes, and Viral Video

There are several ways to understand the significance of viral video itself as an important segment in a broader new media landscape. Certainly technological changes factor into the rise of viral video since the continuing, increasing success of video Web sites like YouTube corresponds to growths in broadband Internet access, to improved encoding technology for streaming video clearly and quickly, and to the proliferation of cameras in society more generally. In addition to these changes in technology, the rise of viral video simultaneously marks a certain sophistication in how users navigate and circulate hypertextual discourse and represents an important evolution in a longstanding phenomenon: the Internet meme.

If there is such a thing as a logic of digitality, then circulation is an important feature of that logic. In other words, most of the basic technologies behind new media technologies (such as binary code and data retrieval) are those that enable users to reproduce, transport, and share stored information in ways that are quicker and more reliable than older analog media forms. This emphasis on portability and exchange is expressed at the end-user level in several ways: hard drives that grow in capacity while shrinking in size, powerful handheld devices like smartphones, the copy and paste feature found in an OS, the "reply all" option found in most e-mail front ends, and so on. All of these developments not only facilitate the circulation of information across multiple texts and contexts, they promote it.

This is important for viral video for several reasons. For one, the very situatedness of viral video on the Web makes it distinct from popular media in other contexts. Viral marketing traditionally anticipated that word of mouth would drive consumer interest, and many advertisers relied on feedback from focus groups, Nielsen ratings, or sales numbers to try and gauge the effect of their commercials (much as politicians relied on poll numbers, filmmakers relied on box office numbers, etc.) Those trying to reach wide audiences with videos that featured novel, pathos-rich appeals often had limited means of ensuring viewership beyond saturating the airwaves at high costs. In addition, not only was the sharing of these videos uncommon with analog media, it also was difficult to accomplish (even dubbing an audio cassette or VHS tape could be a lengthy process and required a *physical* exchange). By contrast, digitality affords the possibility for the users to carry out the work of distribution for those interested in propagating these messages. It also allows for built-in measures to quantitatively and qualitatively track viewership and audience responses that surpass what is available for analog media. For this reason, viral video is only possible in a digital context, it has no exact equivalent in older media.

Second, adopting a nuanced view of circulation and the technology that enables these processes is helpful for understanding how rhetoric functions online. For example, it is wise to consider how the circulation of viral video alters those traditional models of discursively constructed power dynamics as found in traditional mass media. On this point, Jean Baudrillard writes:

> That discourse "circulates" is to be taken literally: that is, it no longer goes from one point to another, but it traverses a cycle that without distinction includes the positions of transmitter and receiver, now unlocatable as such. Thus there is no instance of power, no instance of transmission—power is something that circulates and whose source can no longer be located....The circularization of power, of knowledge, of discourse puts an end any localization of instances and poles. (41)

For Baudrillard, circulation in our fragmented and sped-up postmodern culture is marked just as much by its ability to displace, to dislocate, and to efface as it is by its ability to create shared experiences. This means that any political agency that might be gained through the use of viral video is especially contingent and fleeting, perhaps even more so than would be the case for agency gained through the use of other forms of media. As Baudrillard suggests, circulation in a hypermediated environment is not seizure of power, but rather a release of control. In this view, viral video is *not* necessarily rhizomatic or structured to survive through nodal points of connection and departure. Instead, like a virus, viral video is subject to the rules of herd mentality and to inoculation; they can persist or die off depending on the environment, the target, or the attention given to them by the (Web site) host. This is, in part, why studying a video's uptake becomes much more important than studying its intent or content for those rhetorical critics interested in efficacy or agency.

In addition, more important than determining the best metaphor to use to describe viral videos' circulation is the recognition that it belongs to a larger subset of Internet-based discourse known as memes. Though the term "meme" is usually traced to work in the 1970s by biologist Richard Dawkins and describes self-perpetuation, the study of memes in language has its roots in the study of ancient rhetoric[7] and is presently most often associated with repeating phrases, videos, images, and other discourse on the Internet. Internet memes can teach us much about the relationship between circulation and rhetoric in digital contexts. In some early writing about Internet memes, Garry Marshall suggests that speed, cultural pervasiveness, and an often-preposterous character are constitutive factors of this kind of discourse:

> Memes can appear at much the same time in different parts of the world regardless of geographical and cultural boundaries to exert their effects. It has also been argued that the speed of transmission, and the resulting rapid cascade of memes across the Internet, makes it more difficult to distinguish between the more and less valuable memes (Taylor, 1996). There is a premium on short, catchy memes as opposed to more complex memes such as lengthy stories. Infectiousness assumes an importance far greater than that of attributes that may well have greater long-term value such as utility and authority.

Memes capture the discursive procession of ideas in vibrant, transformative fashion. As Davi Johnson adds, "The meme is in itself a valuable methodological tool that is particularly suited to the analysis of popular culture discourses that transform social practices in spite of their apparent superficiality and triviality," adding "the meme is a particularly suitable tool for analyzing the political effects of cultural currents" (28–29). These currents can be traced by attending to how memetic discourse is taken up across various contexts.

Viral videos are the most recent instance of a practice that has taken place on the Web almost since its inception.[8] As "encyclopedia of all things Internet" WhatPort:80 puts it:

> The meme is kind of a way that the lulz [instances of laughing] had can [*sic*][9] be remembered in the form of OC and happiness spreads throughout the subcultures of the Internet for at least two years before it is considered old and everyone wants to forget about it. Sometimes the meme has nothing to do with lulz but everything to do with regular humour.

In addition, the site provides a timeline of how Internet memes develop, a "lifespan" of sorts. After memes originate and become popularized in their "localized" Web subculture, they begin to spread to "subcultures tolerant of the origin" where they are modified and amplified in new ways until finally attracting widespread notoriety. At the point where memes begin to become co-opted by mainstream Web sites, used in offline communication, and commercialized through "Snorg Tees and Facebook bumper stickers," the originators of the meme gain notoriety and "the meme decays and rots" before being archived on Web culture sites. WhatPort:80's often tongue-in-cheek explanation of memes is essentially an explanation of the hypertemporal, hyperspatial character of much of Internet discourse that Baudrillard alluded to above. The life cycle of the meme teaches us something about its rhetorical significance (and thus that of viral video). That is, embedded in their humorous description of memetic circulation are insights into how memes are often co-opted, taken out of context, and slowly killed through commercialization and prolonged exposure. We saw some of this process unfold in our discussion of the responses to both the Lady Gaga and Christine O'Donnell's videos, and sure enough O'Donnell's witch meme already appears in T-shirt form on zazzle.com.

Conclusion

In this chapter we have discussed the features and functions of viral video, emphasizing how their memetic quality makes them suitable for rhetorical criticism that focuses on circulation and uptake. At this stage, viral video remains a developing form of digital discourse, and its future hinges on both further developments in Web technology and in user acclimation and response. Currently, novelty still seems to factor into any one video's success, but it is not the only indicator of whether a video will "go viral" or what kind of impact it will make with audiences. In the next chapter we will consider these audiences in more detail by discussing the role of intertextuality in shaping meaning for Web users.

Notes

1. Also worth noting is that many of the most popular viral videos get posted multiple times on and across a variety of video-hosting Web sites, making aggregate data collecting a bit cumbersome.
2. MemeMachine's methods for understanding "viral video" parallels traditional methods of assessing the success of "viral marketing," a concept that predates the popularity of YouTube by almost a decade.
3. The Web site also lists such interesting statistics as a "discovered" date and buzz by language, in addition to tracking the sharing of the video over time and the top places where the video is being shared.
4. For scholarship on the rhetoric of film, see work such as Kendall Phillips's *Projected Fears: Horror Films and American Culture* (2005), David Blakesley's *The Terministic Screen: Rhetorical Perspectives on Film* (2007), or David Bordwell's *Making Meaning: Inference and Rhetoric in the Interpretation of Cinema* (1991).
5. See Judith Butler's *Bodies That Matter: On the Discursive Limits of "Sex"* (1993) and *Excitable*

Speech: A Politics of the Performative (1997) for further discussion of the concept of a citational legacy.

6. It is unclear whether the video is actually from someone who considers themselves to be a Klan member, as much of the video is hyperbolic and attempts to be offensive—something that marks both the actual Klan's discourse as well as responses to them.

7. Rhetorical concepts like *epimone* (repeated phrases), *ploce* (repetition with added meaning), and *palilogia* (emphatic redundancy) all address some of the rhetorical strategies associated with memes. For more, see Lanham, *A Handlist of Rhetorical Terms*.

8. For detailed histories of Internet memes, check out the timeline at http://www.dipity.com/tatercakes/Internet_Memes/ and "Greg Rutter's Definitive List of the 99 Things You Should Have Already Experienced on the Internet Unless You're a Loser or Old or Something" (http://youshouldhaveseenthis.com/)

9. The use of "had can" itself refers to the meme "lolcats," which are pictures of cats with accompanying sloppy grammar to mimic "cat speak."

5

Intertextuality and Web-based Public Discourse

On 14 December 2010, the *Huffington Post* presented a parodic video recounting President Obama's many challenges during his first years in office. Comprised of an Obama look-alike (actor Ron Butler) and a large chorus celebrating "Obama's" statements, the video struck a chord with its online viewing audience ("President Obama Defends Himself"). The musical spoof took the form of a "patter song" as exemplified in the nineteenth-century comic opera by Gilbert and Sullivan, "The Pirates of Penzance," which initially debuted in New York City in 1897 (Wikipedia Foundation, *Pirates of Penzance*).

The production of the Obama video spoof serves as a masterful example of an adroit use of intertextuality as a genre because its viewers had to be thoroughly familiar with the political background and preceding chronology of political events in order to fully appreciate the video's content. They also had to have some sense of the genre from which the design of the production originated, as one blogger in the audience commented: "I guess you have to be familiar with Gilbert and Sullivan's comic opera to appreciate this bit!" This comment nicely identifies the video spoof as a "mocking imitation of someone or something, usually light and good humored" ("Spoof"), since it was transformed from comic opera to political parody by means of an actor and chorus's video production, thus becoming a modification of existing artistic material transposed from one form into another.

The content of this parodic production is also intertextual in the sense that it brings to mind the possibility that the presentation itself has multiple potential meanings as we will explain below. As Wikipedia notes, the patter song form of this genre is characterized by a moderate fast to very fast tempo with a rapid succession of rhythmic patterns in which each syllable of text corresponds to one note. It also makes use of rapidly delivered alliterative words and other consonant or vowel sounds that are intended to be entertaining to listen to (Wikimedia Foundation Patter Song).

To follow the content, the audience members had to mentally keep up with the themes introduced and also with the internal parodic allusions added by the speaker and the chorus. Then there is the question of whether the author (spokesman Ron Butler) was satirizing the president by alluding to how he handled his challenges early in his term in office. To determine this, viewers had to be familiar with the discursive context in which the parodic video was developed. The attendant ambiguity as to the video's origin and intent suggests that its content was "double voiced," in that its origin was linked to a comic opera that featured a character who was seemingly well educated and privileged but lacked any useful military knowledge.

Viewer responses were therefore mixed, in that blog correspondents' reactions did not coincide with each other. One viewer took the video as being "very pro-Obama," while others interpreted the production as critical of the president's capacities as a political leader. Respondents in that group viewed the video as a satire of Obama's high opinion of himself. What this suggests is that the intertextual content for this sort of production can be interpreted in various ways, depending on how recipients connect the content with the events and issues that are referenced by its creators.

The content of the Obama musical spoof was threaded through with references to Obama's trials, tribulations, and successes early in his first term in office. For example, remarks about Obama's race:

The chorus: "Although he's black, Joe Biden says he's clean and quite articulate."

And also about the verbal assault on Obama by Representative Joe Wilson during President Obama's health care address to Congress in September 2009.

The chorus: "A congressman lost his control and even said 'You lie' to me."

The Obama character follows this example with the comment, "The only time I lie is when I say I don't smoke cigarettes."

The content of this video therefore illustrated the ways in which intertextuality as a genre is comprised of the cultural matrix of the readers' experience and general knowledge of salient current events supporting the intertextual reference, including allegorical references, the intratextual environment (i.e., the context in which the cross-reference is located), and other instances of parody and satire.

This chapter will focus on the rhetorical dimensions of intertextuality as used on the World Wide Web. It will consider how the presence of intertextuality may contribute to a site's appeal as readers participate in the construction of textual meaning. The chapter will also focus on specific intertextual references as a form of intertextuality, although the term can also apply to broader conceptions of what intertextuality is. Intertextuality is not just cross-reference and allusion between written texts. It also includes responses to the larger cultural context and elements within that context with which readers are likely to be already familiar. This aspect of intertextuality as used in context will be illustrated in some of the examples in this chapter.

Before continuing with discussion of this genre, it is important to note differences between online reading behavior as compared with reading stable print texts. Many extended or complex argumentative forms (with the exception of the enthymeme) require the reader or listener's sustained attention to continuous text or speech. These forms involve reasoning chains in which prior acceptance of earlier claims enables arguers to build on what has been established earlier. Web reading, however, is discontinuous and fragmented; readers read rapidly and piece together what they read from various sources. As Nancy Kaplan has noted, in Web reading, there is no predetermined next node in the reading process, and readers must continually make choices about what to read next. As they read, they proceed by weighing alternatives, constructing forecasts, and then continually modifying their expectations (Kaplan). They are restless. In such an environment, intertextuality has an appeal. It is modular and does not depend on sequenced text. It offers a wide repertoire of ways to engage attention, such as the use of embedded hyperlinks to external resources, as readers become complicit in constructing the meanings of the texts they encounter.

As we have noted, intertextuality depends on the cultural matrix of readers' experience and general knowledge, as well as salient current events known to the public, and also to other texts. These texts may be comprised of the readers' experience and general knowledge, embedded hyperlinks supporting the intertextual reference, allegorical references, or the intratextual environment in which the reference is located. They may also include extratextual events the reader might research or humorous forms such as parody and satire.

The purpose of this chapter is to consider the nature of Web-based intertextuality in relation to its rhetorical function. By focusing on various specific forms of intertextuality and explaining how they function online, the chapter will identify strategies used by Web authors drawing upon intertextuality as a resource.

Likewise, the chapter will consider the probable roles of Web users as readers when they interpret and are influenced by the texts they encounter. After a brief account of the history and use of the term "intertextuality," the chapter will consider the forms it takes and the stages readers go through in textual appropriation. Through use of example texts, we will illustrate how different readers can interpret the same intertextually based text in different ways depending on their prior experiences and awareness of pertinent facts and events. We also will show that one implication of variable reader uptake of intertextual cross-references is that Web authors should consider their likely audiences' knowledge of and interest in public events when they create multimodal, hypertext-based public discourse.

Intertextuality Then and Now

Keep in mind that intertextuality is not a new form of expression, nor is it unique to the Internet. While the term "intertextuality" was coined by Julia Kristeva shortly after she arrived in France in the mid-1960s (Allen), its variations—parody, caricature, allusion, appropriation, and so forth—have been with us for some time. For example, during the medieval period, readers and listeners viewed the literal meaning of scriptural texts as a way to understand deeper meanings. They drew on allegorical interpretive methods to comprehend signs embedded in the text that required interpretation (Soffer). In the early modern and modern periods with the rise of the novel, intertextuality took a different form. Novelists sought to create texts with references drawn from other texts as well as out of the reader's social context, and they depended on the reader's familiarity with other literary works. Graham Allen has noted that these authors did not just select other texts for appropriation but also selected plots, aspects of character, and ways of narrating from previous literary texts and the literary tradition.

Early Conceptions of Intertextuality: Kristeva and Bakhtin

To some extent, Graham Allen is correct to have observed that "intertextuality is one of the most commonly used and misused terms in contemporary critical theory" (2). As we will explain later in this chapter, the term is so unstable that nearly every theorist or critic writing about it defines it in a different way. To say that the term is "misused," however, implies that there is a "correct use" against which other definitions can be gauged, and that appears not to be the case. The best hope for gaining an appreciation for the term's many meanings and applications is to consider the various ways that it has been specified and defined since its inception, and that is what we plan to do.

At the broadest level, one might think of intertextuality as "the fact of one text including various references from another text or texts" (Hitchon and Jura 145). Thus, intertextuality occurs when one text is in some way connected in a work to other texts in the social and textual matrix. There are, however, so many ways in which this can happen that there is little consensus about what constitutes intertextuality. In this section, we plan to begin with the broadest and least limited idea of the term and then proceed to describe versions of intertextuality that are more specific. In light of our purpose in this chapter, we have selected those conceptions that we believe to be the most useful for analyzing the rhetorical workings of intertextuality in Web-based discourse.

As we have noted, the term "intertextuality" first entered the critical lexicon through the work of Julia Kristeva (Allen). Kristeva immigrated to Paris from Eastern Europe where she had been strongly influenced by the writings of Russian literary scholar Mikhail Bakhtin. Both Bakhtin and Kristeva were centrally concerned with the ways in which discourse was presented and experienced in the novel. Bakhtin viewed the novelistic literary word as an "intersection of textual surfaces" (Kristeva 64) that interwove the speech of the writer, the characters, and the ways of speaking of a given period artistically into a narrative whole.

Kristeva believed that the novelist's writing unfolds and faces in two directions—toward the narration of the work and also toward its textual premises (i.e., speech drawn from other texts and the speech context). Her conception of intertextuality growing out of Bakhtin's work thus was diffuse because, in her view, novelistic works were comprised of many voices and texts and were thus multivocal. Like Bakhtin, Kristeva assumed that "any text is constructed as a mosaic of quotations; any text is an absorption and transformation of [other] texts" (66).

This characterization of intertextuality has been widely misunderstood as displacing the author's intended meaning and giving over control of the text's interpretation entirely to the reader (e. g., Irwin). Bakhtin's intent, however, was to de-center the novelist's use of speech and language. He viewed the novelist as one who represents speech, as a writer who "does not speak in a given language (from which he distances himself to a greater or lesser degree), but [who] speaks, as it were, *through* language, a language that has somehow more or less materialized, become objectivized, that he merely ventriloquates" (Bakhtin 299, emphasis original). For Kristeva, then, intertextuality was the space in which "in a given text, several utterances, taken from other texts, intersect and neutralize one another" (36).

This idea might best be understood from an example used by Bakhtin from Charles Dickens' novel *Little Dorrit:*

The conference was held at four or five o'clock in the afternoon, when all the region of Harley Street, Cavendish Square, was resonant of carriage-wheels and double-knocks. It had reached this point when Mr. Merdle came home *from his daily occupation of causing the British name to be more and more respected in all parts of the civilized globe capable of appreciation of wholewide commercial enterprise and gigantic combinations of skill and capital.* For, though nobody knew with the least precision what Mr. Merdle's business was, except that it was to coin money, these were the terms in which everybody defined it on all ceremonious occasions, and which it was the last new polite reading of the parable of the camel and the needle's eye to accept without inquiry. (book 1, ch. 33; cited in Bakhtin 303; emphasis in original)

The first sentence of this passage is a colorful but factual description of the conference site in the author's voice. The italicized speech that follows it is a parodic stylization of formal speeches of the day. Spoken in a ceremonious epic tone, it draws from presumptuous expressions then circulating in the social discourse. The author's voice then returns, only to be interrupted again by a wry aside—"these were terms in which everybody defined it on all ceremonious occasions" (303).

The passage concludes with a specific intertextual allusion to Matthew 19:24 where Jesus said, "It is easier for a camel to go through the eye of a needle than for a rich man to enter the kingdom of God." In this passage, then, the author speaks in his own voice when providing descriptions of narrated contexts and events but then appropriates texts from other sources—officious speech, what "everybody says," the Bible—to represent various points of view. As Bakhtin noted, the novelist's discourse is often thus "another's speech" in "another's language" (313). The adroit use of such speech is what constitutes the artistry of novelistic prose representation. This was Kristeva's view of intertextuality at the time she coined the term.

It may serve us well to think of intertextuality in this broad sense. The Web—and other venues of Internet discourse—are cacophonous environments, sites of Burke's "unending conversation" (*Philosophy* 110) where many voices blend and clash. They are comprised of a network of textual relations where "meaning becomes something which exists between a text and all the other texts to which it refers" (Allen 1). Here all utterances depend on and draw from other utterances, and every expression is shot through with other competing and conflicting voices. While speech on the Web may not emulate the artistry of novelistic prose, it nonetheless represents in itself an unstructured intertextual environment.

In the interest of developing a more highly defined typology of forms of intertextuality found in message texts on the Web, however, we will now turn to definitions by other, subsequent theorists. Our plan is to describe four forms of intertextuality that have been defined in the literature, moving from a general form to other, more specified forms such as hypertextual discourse.

Intertextual Variations

Let us begin with a form of intertextuality that establishes a relation between signs and texts on the one hand and the larger cultural text on the other. This form of relation, labeled by Hitchon and Jura as *archetypal allegory*, is not with a supporting "text" per se but instead with an allegory in which characters or events "represent particular qualities or ideas related to morality, religion, or politics" ("Allegory"). These might be characterized as themes or ideas widely recognized in a culture, and Hitchon and Jura observe that while "the average reader usually does not realize where [allegorical] images come from . . . they are . . . perfectly understandable within a particular culture" (147). That is, culturally specific motifs, knowledges, and beliefs provide the intertext that informs the reader's appreciation and understanding of the intertextually supported text.

An appropriate example of this phenomenon can be found in Robert Scholes's book, *Protocols of Reading*. There he described two images—a painting of two figures and a photograph of a mother giving her daughter a bath. The first of these, titled *The Education of the Virgin*, appears to be an early-seventeenth-century painting in which a girl is reading a book with the aid of large candle held in her left hand. The book she is reading is being held open by a woman with an expression of calm and patience on her face. Although the book cannot be visibly identified, Scholes speculates that it is the Bible and, based on the painting's title, that the child is a visual representation of the Virgin Mary as a child. The second image, captured by an American photographer in Japan in 1972, shows the female figure in the bath as misshapen, with legs as thin as sticks and arms and hands twisted in impossible shapes. Scholes tells us that this image was part of a photo essay that appeared in *Life* magazine of events in a Japanese fishing village that had been saturated with industrial pollution, causing illness and deformities in the local population. The grown child in the bath is being held by her mother, and Scholes notes that her expression is one of "tenderness and love" (27). He maintains that, in the interpretation of both of these images, the Christian allegory plays a role. For the Western reader and across time and space, the bond between mother and child enhances our understanding of the visual texts such that "those of us brought up in the tradition of Christian art read the picture[s] unconsciously, in terms of this cultural code, which conditions our response" (26).

Allegorical motifs frequently provide an intertextual resource for the representation of ideas and themes in online environments. These may be represented in various ways (e.g., as a quest in search of some prized object, sacrifice of a person or thing for some larger value or purpose, or sudden illumination and discovery because of divine intervention). In any case, we can look to allegory as "a specific method of reading a text, in which characters and narrative or descriptive details are taken by the reader as an elaborate metaphor for something outside the literal story" ("Allegory").

A second type of intertextual reference that complements *archetypal allegory* is cross-reference to a *specific film, novel, or other work* that is widely known and recognized by readers and media consumers. One example of this type is the now-famous 1984 Super Bowl television advertisement for the Apple Macintosh computer that was about to be released (Hitchon and Jura). The spot opens with men, apparently in prison garb, marching in lockstep formation into an auditorium where a black and white projection of a threatening, authoritative male figure intones a speech on "Information Purification" and "Unification of Thoughts." Suddenly, a youthful, strong woman in bright red shorts and shoes runs into the auditorium pursued by storm troopers and hurls a sledgehammer at the screen, which then explodes. Then, a calm voice intones that "On January 24th, Apple computer will introduce Macintosh. And you'll see why 1984 won't be like '1984'" (Apple).

As Hitchon and Jura observe, viewers unfamiliar with George Orwell's novel *1984* and its account of an oppressive police state and limits on free speech would have been unable to fully appreciate the advertisement's message (150). They also note that IBM's then-dominant monopoly of the computing market as represented by the persona on the screen was an aspect of the social context supporting the advertisement's message and would have contributed to understanding and uptake of the persuasive aspect of the text's message.

In her study of the ad, Sarah R. Stein noted further possible intertextual cross-references to specific works in this famous advertisement. The opening shot of the marching workers was reminiscent of the 1927 film *Metropolis* that depicted capitalistic oppression and the misery of the working class. The running woman in the ad (the sole colorful figure in a black and white environment) represented "a political figure, one aware of the repressive powers of advanced capitalism and willing to use revolutionary tactics in response" (S. Stein 187). The sledgehammer wielding episode and the shattered image of the authoritarian figure on the screen suggested a female David in confrontation with a corporate Goliath. In addition, the bleak landscape of the marching figures and the docile workers in air thick with smog and haze seems visually reminiscent of Ridley Scott's 1982 science fiction film *Blade Runner*.

A third and commonly recognized form of intertextuality is *parody*, defined as "discursive activity"that intentionally copies the style of someone famous or copies a particular situation, making the features or qualities of the original more noticeable in a way that is humorous" ("Parody"). Such a definition implies intentionally explicit or implicit juxtaposition of two texts that is contrived by an author who places a popular or known text in relation to another text and that imitates or exaggerates the "original" text. One example of this can be found in Warnick's 2002 book, *Critical Literacy in a Digital Era* where a text from George W. Bush's 2000 campaign homepage is parodied by another parody site that mocks the Bush site's then well-known welcoming statement. The text from the Bush homepage is as follows:

> Welcome to georgewbush.com—my virtual campaign headquarters. The most important question I can answer for you is why I am running for President of the United States. I am running for President because our country must be prosperous. But prosperity must have a purpose. The purpose of prosperity is to make sure the American dream touches every willing heart. The purpose of prosperity is to leave no one out— to leave no one behind. I'm running because my political party must match a conservative mind with a compassionate heart. And I'm running to win. (Bush for President).

The bushlite parody site capitalized on this official homepage text by incorporating its style and word choice into a fabricated announcement speech said to have been given in June 1999:

> Prosperity is not a given. That wouldn't be prosperous, nor would it have a purpose. What's the purpose of giving out prosperity to just anyone? Purposeful prosperity— that is prosperity with a purpose—must be earned. To earn it, we need compassionate conservatism. By this I mean conservatism that is also compassionate. (DieTryin.com)

While capitalizing on the euphemistic quality and circularity of the "original" Bush homepage statement, this parody text imports the idea that prosperity must be "earned" through "compassionate conservatism," which is nonetheless not intended for everyone but only for those who "earn" it.

A fourth type of intertextual usage is that which explicitly takes up and plays upon the larger social text. This type of intertextuality frequently takes the form of satire, in which "the humor, irony, exaggeration, or ridicule is used so as to expose and criticize people's stupidity or vices, particularly in the context of contemporary politics and other topical issues" ("Satire"). *Intertextual satire* is a common form of online expression that draws upon situations widely covered in the news or familiar texts produced elsewhere in the media environment. In other words, intertextual satire often draws upon well-recognized phenomena to lampoon an individual.

An example of this form can be seen in a *Huffington Post* collage of Sara Palin parodies, posted on February 11, 2011. The *Post*'s introduction to the suite of parody clips ran as follows:

> On Today, February 11, exactly 47 years ago, a baby girl was brought into the world with no idea she'd someday become Governor of Alaska, a Vice-Presidential nominee, or one of politics' greatest gifts to comedy since George W. Bush.
>
> To honor her 47 years, and the two of those years in which she's enhanced the world of comedy, we present to you exactly 47 seconds of her best parodies. From Sara Benincasa, Liz Cackowski, Mercy Malick, Tina Fey, Gina Gershon. (*Huffington Post.com*, "Happy 47th Birthday")

In the first clip, the first Palin lookalike says, "An older gentleman (John McCain lookalike) called me on the phone and said, 'Would you be my vice president?" Standing at her front door when he turns up, she replies, "I have to go pick up my daughter at hockey practice and I got a lasagna in the oven!" A later clip shows an officious questioner asking, "Are there parts of the country you consider un-American?" She replies: "Yes; New York, New Jersey, Massachusetts, Connecticut, Delaware, and California!" One of the last clips shows her about to play an instrument in a competition but pausing to ask, "Oh, are we not doing the talent portion?"

This example expresses some interesting aspects of intertextual satire. By its pure existence, satire reminds an audience of past events and puts them in a frame. For example, in response to the "the 47th birthday suite," viewing audiences are likely to recall Tina Fey's biting critiques of Palin when she was running for vice president with John McCain; Palin's tendency to answer questions hurriedly and with little forethought; and her background as a homemaker and mother. (It is worth noting that, despite Fey's satirizing impressions of Palin, the two women joined together on a later episode of *Saturday Night Live* to provide comic commentary on the larger political scene.)

This description of four forms of intertextuality reveals some of the many ways in which readers themselves play a role in the construction and interpretation of meaning. Understanding and appreciation of the two images in Scholes's description would be enhanced when the images are interpreted allegorically. The Macintosh advertisement was planned so as to be interpreted in light of Orwell's novel, and the parodic speech attributed to "bushlite" could only have been fully appreciated as a parody when read in intertextual relation to the welcome message on the official 2000 Bush campaign site. The examples of the Palin parodies effectively illustrate the connection between users' knowledge of an individual's public actions and the means by which satire can function as ridicule by drawing on awareness of audience knowledge about past events.

Readers, then, play a role in supplying textual readings; they are active participants in the formation of meaning in the texts they encounter. Furthermore, this is a rhetorical process because the more allusions and cross-references the reader gets, the greater is that reader's sense of accomplishment. As Ott and Walter observe:

> Examining such cultural knowledge fosters feelings of superiority and belonging. Since not all [readers] will recognize the allusions, successful identification of parodic references allows readers to mark themselves as . . . literate. . . . The pleasure of recognition is often directly proportional to the difficulty of identifying the allusion. (436)

The next section of this chapter will consider how reader reception occurs in intertextual hypertext by explaining how readers encounter sites and make intertextual connections when consuming them.

The Reader and the Intertext

In thinking about the reader's role in interpreting intertextual relations, it is useful to consider Roland Barthes' concepts of readerly and writerly texts. Influenced by Kristeva's account of intertextuality, Barthes emphasized the extent to which the reader plays a role in the formation and comprehension of texts, and he demonstrated that the conventional view of the author as sole origin and generator of meaning was a false one. This author-centered view implied the idea of a readerly text as one in which the reader is positioned as relatively passive—a figure whose task is to follow the predetermined storyline until a truth, presumed to lie behind the narrated events, is unfolded before him or her (Allen). Thus, the "readerly text" is one in which the reader is to be only that—a consumer of the text as designed by the author.

Instead, Barthes viewed the text not as the unique and original creation of an author but rather as "made up of multiple meanings, drawn from many cultures, and entering into multiple relations of dialogue, parody, contestation, [and] there is one place where this multiplicity is focused and that is the reader, not, as was hitherto said, the author" (148). The reader in Barthes's view thus became "that *someone* who holds together in a single field all the traces by which the written text is constituted" (148). The inveterately intertextual text (as opposed to the unified work) "grows by vital expansion, by 'development' (a word which is significantly ambiguous, at once biological and rhetorical); the metaphor of the Text is that of the *network*; if the Text extends itself, it is as a result of a combinatory systematic" (161).

This insistence on text as an open, networked system that can be appropriated by readers in various ways introduces some noticeable tensions that must be negotiated in thinking about the workings of intertextuality. If authors and producers design texts so as to be taken up in certain ways by virtue of how they are structured and designed, what role, if any, does the originator of the text have in the interpretations of its meaning? If hypertext productions can be read in any order and connected with other texts in numerous ways, do the authors of Web-based discourse function as authors at all in the traditional sense?

Our response to this question aligns with Allen's who, at the end of his long study of theories of intertextuality, concluded that "hypertext makes author, text, and reader into joint participants of a plural, intertextual network of significations and potential significations" (202). It is the case, as we will show in this chapter, that both producers and users of Web-based discourse play a role in the constitution of meaning. In most cases of intentionally rhetorical discourse, however, online authors endeavor to canalize their readers' interpretations, but they often do so in such a way that users have a role in the process. Or, as Ott and Walter put it, "Some texts . . . deploy intertextuality as a stylistic device in a manner that shapes how audiences experience those texts" (434).

That said, readers nevertheless play a strong role in taking in the texts they encounter, and the question then becomes, how do they do this? It might be helpful here to consider Stuart Hall's tripartite model for how different groups of readers interpret media texts. This includes "dominant reading" in which the reader fully shares the text's code; "negotiated meaning," in which the reader partly shares the text's code but sometimes resists it; and "oppositional reading," where the reader rejects the text's code and brings to bear an alternative frame of reference (Hall (33)). As will be seen in this chapter's case studies, users often encounter sites combining parody, satire, pastiche, general allusions to cultural contexts, and other forms of intertextuality. In interpreting these texts, users must be able to make sense of what they encounter. After all, if the content makes no sense to them, they are likely to break off their reading and viewing and leave the site, so the question of how they make sense of what they see is an important question insofar as the possible rhetorical influence of messages is concerned.

Intertextual Content and Reader Reception

In thinking about how users as readers process the texts they encounter, one might turn to a general account of meaning making in hypermodal environments proposed by Jay L. Lemke. He maintained that there are three semiotic functions that play a role in users' responses to Web-based discourse. The first depends on *presentational* meanings, which enable users to construe a state of affairs from what is said, shown, or portrayed on the site. Operationally, one might say that this is the phase of meaning making in which the user, when initially looking at the site, could answer the question "What is this about?"

The second function depends on *orientational* meaning, which enables users to orient to the communication situation in terms of point of view. In this phase, a user would be able to answer such questions as "What is being asked of me?" and "How am I being treated or positioned?" Lemke noted that factors such as terms of address as well as the mood or modality of expression work as orientation indicators.

The third function is comprised of *organizational* meaning, which enables users to determine which signs go together into larger units. Display patterns such as image groupings, link menus, and sites' graphic identity facilitate the users' development of organizational meanings.

In applying this framework to his analysis of two Web sites, Lemke makes it clear that meaning making is an emergent process that commences when the user first encounters the site and then develops his or her understanding based on signs, pathways, forms of expression, and representations encountered on the site. He notes that the three functions are not independent of one another and that we, as users

> recognize patterns by parallel processing of information of different kinds from different sources ... and we refine our perceptions and interpretations as we notice and integrate new information into prior patterns in ways that depend in part on our having already constructed those prior, now provisional patterns. (305)

Lemke's account of meaning making here applies especially well to Web-based discourse that evidences a good deal of intertextuality. Sites of commentary, resistance, and political parody, as well as entertainment sites involving social criticism may not be immediately understandable to all users.

Being able to identify the relevant intertexts that enable users to understand what is being said is a vital component in the success of persuasive communication on these sites. Since different readers possess different levels of textual knowledge on various topics, they will read and appreciate the same text differently (Ott and Walter). Producers of such sites also need to negotiate a tension between making their content so accessible that it lacks originality and uniqueness on one hand and, on the other hand, developing content with allusions that are so arcane and specialized as not to be understandable.

To this point, then, we have reviewed various types of intertextual discourse, identifying them and discussing the allegorical forms that provide commentary and perspective on the larger social context, as well as films and videos that draw upon cross-references to well-known films and other works recognized by readers and parodies that play upon current texts and situations so as to make their features more noticeable by means of imitation.

Intertextuality also abounds in satire, a genre designed to expose the foibles and shortcomings of well-known individuals by revealing their weaknesses and oversights. In all these cases, the readers play a role in interpretation and construction of meaning by tacitly supplying the implied but unstated content based on their own knowledge of events and situations.

Users' participation in the ongoing assimilation of textual content provides opportunities for them to position themselves as new political subjects by articulating the elements of existing phenomena and by forming linkages between their components and coming to understand the effects of such linkages. Stuart Hall has spoken of articulation along these lines, observing that, while "articulate" means to "speak forth," to be articulate, it also carries the sense of language-ing, of expressing, etc. But, he notes, we also speak of an "articulated lorry (truck): a lorry where the front and back can . . . but need not necessarily, be connected to one another. The two parts are connected to each other, but through a specific linkage that can be broken. (*Hall Critical Dialogues* (53).

An articulation is thus the form of the connection that *can* make a unity of two different elements, under certain conditions. It is a linkage that is not necessary, determined, absolute and essential. The so-called unity of a discourse is really the articulation of different, distinct elements that can be rearticulated in different ways because they have no necessary "belonging-ness" (Hall, 53).The 'unity" that matters is a linkage between that articulated discourse and the social forces with which it can, under certain historical conditions but not necessarily, be connected.

Thus, a theory of articulation is both a way of understanding how ideological elements come,under certain conditions, to cohere together within a discourse, and a way of asking how they do or do not become articulated, at specific conjunctures, to certain political subjects. Hall concludes by saying that a theory of articulation "enables us to think about how an ideology empowers peoples, enabling them to begin to make some sense or intelligibility of their historical situation without reducing those forms of intelligibility to their socio-economic class or social position" (53).

It is by this means that satirists, parodists, and commentators often succeed in reshaping public perceptions of current events by exposing features that would otherwise go unnoticed.

Jibjab.com: Intertextuality at Work

To illustrate the role and effectiveness of skillful use of allusions in intertextual parody, one can surely look to innovative presentations of political parody such as is found on the Web site *JibJab.com*. Historically this site has produced parodies of commentary on the political scene, including the 2004 production "This Land," intended to lampoon the political campaigns of both George Bush and John Kerry. JibJab is a digital entertainment studio based in Venice, California, and was founded by Evan and Gregg Spiridellis in 1999 (Wikipedia). Their initial 2004 animation was followed up by the 2–0-0–5 year in review parody of the Bush presidency, including characters such as Mahmoud Ahmadinejad, Scooter Libby, and Tom Delay (Wikipedia JibJab).

Subsequent parodies were devised and presented in later years, but probably the best example so far is "So Long to Ya, 2010." This was composed as a Barack Obama and Joe Biden duet; they lamented their respective challenges and misfortunes during Obama's second year in office. In their own report on the creation of this animation, the Spiridellis brothers and their Web team compiled a fast-moving list of events that occurred during the year. They started off with a focus on Obama, but as the project developed, they decided that the Obama character was having a hard time carrying the song ("The Daring Young Man on the Flying Trapeze"), so they came up with the idea of adding in Joe Biden as Obama's sidekick, which, they say, "opened up a whole universe of new gags."(JibJab, "The Writing Process").

The song begins with Obama and Biden noting,

"We arrived in '09 on a rainbow of hope,
"but two thousand ten blew it all up in smoke.
"From Tea Party Rallies to banks going broke [bank building collapses around Obama],
So long to ya two thousand ten!"
Obama sings in referring to the year:
"You brought no jobs despite all my spending [while he throws dollar bills at the audience].
We passed health care, they shouted 'Repeal!'
"So old Joe went on national TV and said,
"IT'S A REAL BIG [BLEEPING] ing DEAL!"

Then there's a host of other problems, including the BP Oil spill that "gushed for 12 [bleep] in' weeks," and that occurred only three weeks after President Obama had announced support for offshore drilling, thus opening up U.S. coastal waters to oil and gas exploration for the first time in more than twenty years.

The song continues, noting other problems: "From Mosques at Ground Zero to damn Wikileaks": "So long to ya two thousand ten." (The reader may recall the widespread controversy regarding whether building a mosque near Ground Zero was appropriate.) A CBS Poll posted in August 2010 found that 71% of responders thought that building the mosque there was inappropriate (CBS News Poll).

The song continues with a grim solo by the Obama character who maintains:

"I passed finance reform, placed a justice (Sotomayor).
"Yet my ratings they plunged through the floor
"I got Rangel, McChrystal and Karzai (not the best threesome),
"And no credit for ending a war!"

Other developments include Michelle's vacation in August that CBS Evening News described as not the "quiet mother-daughter trip the first lady would have been able to take as a private figure," because many details of the trip such as Secret Service agents and use of Transport on the Air Force version of a 757 ($146,000 for the round trip) were made public though news reports. Her jaunt cost taxpayers a good amount, and the *New York Daily News* called the first lady "Marie Antoinette" (CBS Interactive).

Given these developments, it's not surprising that our duet had little regard for the year in review:

"Oh two thousand ten, we can't wait for you,
"To jet like that guy from Jet Blue!"[as they momentarily slide down an escape ramp].

The final lament of the video sums up the situation nicely.

"Inherited wars, and mountains of debt.
"Gridlocked politicians and nuclear threats.
"As President that seems to be what you get . . ."
Obama: "That's why I want one—"
Biden: "He only wants one—!"
"Just give me a damn cigarette!"[At which point the Obama character is knocked off his perch by a flying basketball.]

This was a reference to Obama's injury to his lip while playing basketball with friends at Fort McNair in November 2010 (Bradley and Smith). This video illustrates the extent to which viewers who follow politics and news reportage will be positioned to be more fully entertained than those who do not. The lyrics bring to mind the many imbroglios that plagued 2010, including the Deepwater Horizon Explosion in the Gulf, the security breaches that followed Wikileaks disclosures, the Middle East conflicts in Iraq, Pakistan, and Afghanistan, including the dismissal of Army General McChrystal from his command, and other signal events of the year.

One of these events alluded to in the video was the incident in which the Jet Blue airline steward, Steven Slater, who, after chiding a passenger for not staying in her seat, was hit by her bag in the face and cursed. He then went to the intercom, chided all the passengers, deployed the plane's inflatable emergency slide, and summarily left the plane at JFK airport. Although he was sentenced to seven years for criminal mischief, he became a Facebook hero for some employees, presumably because they identified with his on-the-job difficulties and sympathized with his situation (Joy).

Intertextuality, Parody, and Social Criticism

JibJab's animations are not limited to entertaining commentary on the political scene, however. They have also undertaken commentary on larger social issues, as evidenced in animations such as "What We Call the News" (in 2007), "He's Barack Obama" (in 2009), and the one we're about to discuss: "Big Box Mart" (in 2005), which is intended as a parody of the marketing practices of the Walmart chain of consumer goods. That this video was still posted on the JibJab site in spring 2011 implies that its creators view it as a viable piece of social commentary on the impacts of capitalistic enterprise and its effects on workers and consumers.

This JibJab video well illustrates the role of satiric videos in activating public understanding of significant issues. As our discussion of Stuart Hall's views on the role of articulation in public understanding of context has illustrated, "intertextuality" does not only refer to relations between written or spoken texts per se; it also can be used to enhance the intelligibility of the larger social context.

The video to be described below illustrates how this functions. By presenting the public with an example of a large enterprise that seems convenient, but nonetheless exploits its employees and offers problematic merchandise, this JibJab video production reveals how intertextual satire and parody can unveil practices that might otherwise go unnoticed.

Walmart has been subject to a number of criticisms, including its tendency to move into locations, provide low-cost items, and displace existing businesses. There have been other problems for the company as well. A 2011 article on the company posted in the *New York Times* Business Day section on 30 March 2011, recounted a number of actions against the company as well as a series of criticisms about its practices.The article noted that the company's pricing policies do enable lower-income households to acquire the goods and services they would not be able to afford otherwise. However, in part, this low pricing has been made possible by exporting manufacturing jobs to foreign countries.

Reliance by domestic companies on the import of goods from other countries is a controversial and troublesome issue for the U.S. economy. A report by the Economic Policy Institute noted that increases in such imports reduce jobs because the imports displace goods that otherwise would have been made in the United States by domestic workers and then exported abroad (Scott). The report noted that the United States has experienced steadily growing global trade deficits since the mid-1990s due to the tendency to import goods produced elsewhere at lower costs rather than producing goods domestically and exporting them outside the United States. The report notes that "in every case, many more jobs are lost due to growing imports than are gained by increasing exports." The report concludes, "All 50 states and the District of Columbia have experienced a net loss of jobs under the North American Free Trade Agreement" (Scott). With this in mind, it is worth noting that Walmart's practice of consistently importing cheaper goods is objectionable to many observers.

While its marketing practices allowed the company to grow stronger during the 2008 recession while the economy as a whole was becoming weaker, Walmart has at the same time acquired a "public relations record that is decidedly mixed" (*New York Times*, Business Day). In 2008, the company agreed to pay more than $352 million to settle lawsuits across the country that claimed it had forced employees to work off the clock. This settlement has been described as "the largest settlement ever for lawsuits over wage violations" (*New York Times*, Business Day).

As of March 2011, Walmart was trying to overturn a class-action suit filed on behalf of more than a million women who claimed that the company had systematically paid them less than men, giving them smaller raises, and offering them fewer opportunities for promotion (*New York Times*, Business Day). This lawsuit was subsequently turned down by the Supreme Court in June 2011.

Well before these developments occurred, however, the folks at JibJab had taken the measure of Walmart. In 2005, they produced an animation parody that highlighted the company's attractions as well as its exploitive practices. The video opens with a cheerful repeat customer who says he always goes to Big Box Mart because it is "the place to buy all of my crap." He says he likes to go there for the cheapest crap with its discounts guaranteed.

But the next day at his workplace, the news was very grim. He learned his job was outsourced to Beijing. He then gets a job at Big Box Mart sweeping "aisle number 9." And cleaning toilets "till they stick me in the grave" (JibJab Media). What is the moral to this story? This is what the chorus has to say:

> "Oh Big Box Mart, my pay check reminds me
> "Your everyday low prices have a price; they aren't free!!!"

What intertextual allusions in these lyrics alert readers to a social problem that some may already recognize and others might not? (It's worth recognizing that audience reception of intertextually based commentary is malleable, since different audiences may interpret the content variably, depending on their prior knowledge and experience). The initially jovial spokesman reminds readers that the goods come from a sweatshop in a foreign factory and end up in Big Box Mart where shoppers buy them on the cheap. But there's a cost to a system where cheap goods aren't cheap, as the fix that he finds himself in at the end of his own endgame reveals.

This sort of social parody that reveals shoppers' tendency to buy cheap goods acquired through exploitation of domestic and foreign workers has the capacity to raise consciousness among audiences sensitive to the anomalies and idiosyncrasies of public culture. Why do U.S. shoppers patronize opportunities that might seem attractive in the short run but at the same time undermine the domestic economy long term?

The "text" here is not only the lyrics of the animation; the "text" includes the larger social context in which some consumer practices are dysfunctional in light of their long-term effects on the good of the polis as a whole. Some admirers of this domestic parody might recognize this; others might merely find the piece entertaining and miss the point.

In any case, this example illustrates the potential for intertextually based parody to reframe audiences' perceptions of complex phenomena and their implications for the systemic good. That this animation has sustained its appeal and popularity with the online audience is testament to the capacity for online parody to take up domestic issues and appeal to audiences that might otherwise have been apathetic and less inclined to readily appreciate the significance and effects of their actions.

Conclusion

Intertextuality's major rhetorical benefit comes from its use of resources in the larger intertext to involve the user in construction of the text's meaning. In some instances, intertextual references function in the same way as enthymemes did in Aristotle's rhetorical logic. Orators historically have used enthymemes as a form of artistic proof; they have involved their audiences in persuasion by drawing on existing premises and special topics known in the host culture to construct their arguments (Kennedy). When Aristotle said that "rhetoric . . . is an ability, in each [particular] case, to see the available means of persuasion" (Kennedy 36), one of the "means" to which he was referring was the orator's familiarity with known and accepted probabilities that furnished the materials for proof in support of rhetorical arguments.

In a more or less similar way, authors of online commentary, parody, and satire rely on familiar events, known texts, culturally specific allegories, and other components of the cultural intertext to produce discourses meaningful to various audiences. "More or less similar" because, unlike audiences of oratory in Aristotle's time, contemporary users of Web-based discourse have at their fingertips resources that enable them to seek out information in the moment in order to more fully understand and appreciate an intertextual reference. Thus, an observation recently made by David Natharius that "the more we know, the more we see" (241) holds true. That is, the more literate users are about current events, art forms, and cultural commonplaces, the more they will see and understand. But because intertextuality on the Web may pique user interest and curiosity and because the Web itself offers nearly unlimited opportunities for finding information, it could also be the case that the more users see, the more they will come to know.

6

Identity, Identification, and Social Media

In chapter 2 we discussed the Web site TeaPartyNation.com and focused on the tools available on the site for users to attempt to construct their own identity within the Tea Party Nation's Web-based social network. TeaPartyNation.com is, of course, only a single example of a much larger twenty-first century phenomenon: the growth of social-networking Web sites and social media.[1] In fact, TeaPartyNation's user base of roughly 40,000 members is quite minimal compared to the user base of social media giants such as Facebook.com (more than 500 million accounts), Myspace.com (60 million), Linkedin.com (over 100 million), or Twitter.com (200 million) ("Statistics"; "DoubleClick Ad Planner"; Weiner; Shiels). More important, these more popular sites are not aligned with a particular ideology or political-party platform; they are ostensibly nonpolitical and offer a more complex set of tools for users and critics alike to take into consideration.

Nonetheless, many of the basic ideas presented earlier about how and why people use social-networking sites for political purposes still apply to these large, "nonpolitical" Web sites. For example, the idea that social networking is a tool that can be used to both construct and defer one's identity and subjectivity is significant when considering the experience of all forms of social media. Lev Manovich's argument that "interactive media asks us to identify with someone else's mental structure" (61) is just as resonant if that mental structure is comprised of family photos and humorous wall postings on Facebook as if it were evidenced through sign-ing tea party meet-up boards or writing right-wing blog posts on TeaPartyNation.com. In other words, even though we have briefly considered how social-networking tools allow users to create specific kinds of identities on politi-cal sites, we have also laid the groundwork for understanding some of the functions and limitations found in any form of social networking, including Facebook or Twitter. This chapter will further investigate how social media operate across a range of cultural practices.

This chapter identifies some of the ways in which rhetorical theory can be used to engage this growing phenomenon. That is, even though social media's high level of cultural penetration is a relatively recent event, there is already a wealth of ideas across the history of rhetorical theory and criticism that can help us to under-stand what is significant about the various practices that take place within these spe-cialized networks of users. Specifically, in this chapter we draw on ideas from Kenneth Burke, Maurice Charland, and other rhetoricians in order to consider the role of rhetoric in social media. Our aim in doing so is to highlight several differ-ent critical concepts and approaches from rhetorical studies that collectively explore multiple facets of social media and social networking. In our view, choosing a sin-gle framework for studying these sites is as limiting as choosing a single framework for studying the Web itself. Instead, as we have done at other points in this text, we wish to emphasize how rhetorical theory can contribute to our understanding of some specific functions of social media by offering several ongoing observations and related critical considerations.

Facilitating Identification: Creating Audiences with Social Media

That Facebook and other social media could become such an important player in contemporary public and private life was something that few could foresee even a few years before Facebook became wildly popular.[2] The speed at which social media have grown in numbers and in significance is faster than many scholars have been able to track, and only recently have we begun to see useful research trends emerge.

Unsurprisingly, recent research on social networking has focused on the 2008 U.S. presidential election that some have dubbed the "Facebook Election." The jour-nal *Mass Communication and Society* featured a special issue in 2010 that examined the role of social networking in the 2008 election. Many media outlets called on experts in media theory to explain the role of social media in that campaign, and several recent books have touched on the role of social media in the campaign or in culture at large; examples would include the edited collections *Facebook and Philosophy* (Wittkower) and *A Networked Self: Identity, Community, and Culture on Social Network Sites* (Papacharissi), as well as projects such as Nancy Baym's *Personal Connections in the Digital Age* and Jesse Rice's *The Church of Facebook: How the Hyperconnected Are Redefining Community*. These resources are valuable for anyone trying to consider social networking from a critical perspective, but there is little across these texts that specifically deals with the role of social networking from the perspective of rhetorical theory.

Across much of this scholarship is the central idea that the 2008 election was the first time that social media became something worth paying attention to. As Johnson and Perlmutter explained, social media "changed the way candidates campaigned, how the media covered the election, and how voters received information" (375). How and why this particular media technology at this particular time was able to capture the public's imagination is worth considering. How did candidates use social media to generate interest and raise funds when their traditional methods for crafting appeals, such as television ads and stump speeches, don't translate well to a social media context? Can a candidate translate a substantial following in social media into election day success at the polls? How might voters use social networking technologies to help them select a candidate? We propose that one potential answer to these questions lies in the relationship between social networking sites and a logic of rhetorical identification.

Kenneth Burke is perhaps best known for his expansion of the definition of rhetoric to encompass identification. This expansion answers the critiques he leveled against the limits of "persuasion" and provides for rhetorical criticism to better engage more than the speech or written word. Specifically, Burke suggested that identification entails "changing a thing's nature," and he focused on how rhetoric creates shifts in attitude. He wrote in *A Rhetoric of Motives*

> As for the relation between "identification" and "persuasion": we might well keep it in mind that a speaker persuades an audience by the use of stylistic identifications; his act of persuasion may be for the purpose of causing the audience to identify with the speaker's interests; and the speaker draws on identification of interests to establish rapport between himself and his audience. (46)

This formulation was concurrent with Burke's interest in early twentieth-century psychology; if persuasion is conscious rhetoric, identification is unconscious rhetoric. Identification allows for the possibility of self-persuasion or creative participation with a text.

Linked to Burke's notion of identification is the term "consubstantiality." Consubstantiality is discussed as "an acting-together; and in acting together, men [*sic*] have common sensations, concepts, images, ideas, attitudes, that make them consubstantial" (21). For this reason, identification works through association: the rhetor attempts to associate some substantive part of himself or herself with the same part in the members of their audience. The result, if effective, is that an audience begins to "feel" as the rhetor feels or to "see the world" from the perspective of the speaker. When these commonalities are established, resistance against changing attitudes or toward pursuing action is lowered. Taking the idea of consubstantiality to its limit, Burke suggests that "in pure identification, there would be no strife" (25).

Burke's positing of "identification" allows rhetorical critics to focus on aspects of the world that are not easily critiqued through a framework of classical "persuasion." For instance (and as suggested by Burke) a theory of rhetoric as identification helps to better account for the way in which fascism operates, gains support from a nation, and is able to succeed in carrying out actions that, through a lens of persuasion, seem especially irrational. A theory of identification is also useful to consider how many media texts (such as films, Web pages, etc.) achieve popularity at certain cultural moments or build fan communities.

A notion of identification can thus be used to consider how one enters into subcultures. Specifically, when considering something like Dick Hebdige's "style" through the lens of "rhetoric as identification," it becomes possible to understand how style is but one component of a process of identification; choosing to wear clothes that mark one as belonging to a group is indicative of consubstantiality occurring at other levels (e.g., shared political ideologies). This same idea is echoed in the discussion of TeaPartyNation.com's social-networking site in chapter 2; users choose to mark themselves as belonging to a group they identify with. Burke clarifies:

> Here is perhaps the simplest case of persuasion. You persuade a man [*sic*] only insofar as you can talk his language by speech, gesture, tonality, order, image, attitude, idea, *identifying* your ways with his (55, emphasis added).

For Burke, rhetorical identification is something that works when an audience feels that they share the same worldview and life experiences as the rhetor. The rhetor, therefore, must use the tools available in order to facilitate this feeling of mutuality.

Social-networking sites and the tools available therein provide a unique exercise in Burkean identification. Specifically, most sites are designed around the idea that users can discover new friends or make new connections with existing ones by sharing their interests, hobbies, political affiliations, or other kinds of personal information from their profile page. Facebook, for example, suggests new friends to users based on tracking their networks or the number of acquaintances that they have in common with existing friends. Users can also easily see how many people in their network share the same "liked" interests through Facebook's profile pages. This basic formula also works with the hashtag system on Twitter or with the specialized interest groups available on sites like Linkedin or Myspace.

The power of identification as a method for self-promotion across social media is something that hasn't been lost on advertisers or political campaigns. An example of each can help us understand how social media might function in a Burkean frame.

Social Pizza

Some of the most successful corporate campaigns in social media have been run by pizza companies. Domino's Pizza, a company with a longstanding Web presence, has found that their use of social-networking sites generated a significant amount of traffic to both the company's Internet and physical stores. For example, in England in 2010 the company's e-commerce grew by more than 60%, making online orders responsible for almost one-third of its total business in that country ("Domino's Finds"). Part of this success is based on their use of Facebook, where the main Domino's page has more than 2 million "likes," but it also comes from their innovative uses of other social media such as Foursquare (Montgomery), their direct engagement with critics and fans alike via Twitter (McDevitt), and their own blog site ("More Domino's"), which includes news that visitors can comment on, games that can be played to earn coupons, and a variety of other ways to interact with Domino's Pizza.

Part of what has made Domino's online success story one that illustrates the logic of identification is the strategy they have used to advertise their pizza. Probably the most important step they have taken is to emphasize Domino's charitable and humanitarian work. Domino's has used social media to raise money for homelessness in Australia ("Something for Nothing!"), for cancer care in Ireland ("Domino's Charity Cycle"), and for St. Jude's Children's Hospital (Anderson), among other causes. Users of social media who donate or otherwise participate in the campaigns are given the option of sharing their experiences automatically via their own personal news feed, which enables users in their network to see that they have done something for charity and that they have taken part in Domino's campaign. The identification at work here is twofold: social media users can identify themselves with the causes that Domino's as a company espouses (thus making their patronage of Domino's more likely), and they can also identify with those in their network who have engaged in the same actions or who have an interest in the same charities.

Papa John's, another international chain that boasts more than 1.5 million "likes" on their Facebook page has also used social media to facilitate identification between themselves, their customers, and their customer's social network. Perhaps their keenest method for accomplishing this is to make it seem like customers and their opinions are vital to the very operation of Papa John's. For example, in the summer of 2010, the company used Facebook and Twitter while promoting a contest to invent a new kind of pizza; royalties and other prizes would be given to the winner. As part of the submission process on Facebook, users had to "like" Papa John's Pizza. Over the summer, they received more than 12,000 submissions by people who were hopeful that they might have a chance at the prize money and their pizza permanently added to the company's menu (Voight). After finalists were selected, the company also encouraged online voting (and ordering) of the pizzas as well as continued "liking" of and posting about Papa John's Pizza. Much as was the case with Domino's charitable campaigns, Papa John's contest generated distinct communities of users who associated themselves with the company and identified with each other by submitting, voting, and otherwise participating in the contest.

Papa John's also uses Twitter to facilitate identification, as their main Twitter account page includes "following" links to accounts of approximately 100 chains from around the world, where customers can interact with the stores in their local neighborhood directly in order to see how parts of the chain might share in the events of their community. For example, Twitter account "PapaJohnsMiami" is the main account for stores in and around Miami, Florida. In their feed they make references to local sports teams (e.g., a tweet from May 1, 2011—"#HEAT Playoffs looking great today @ halftime. Order any LG Pizza tonight for only $12 @ www.papajohns.com. Let's Go Heat!"), news stories, weather (e.g., a tweet from December 2009—"HEAVY RAIN in MIAMI. Stay Dry! Order an XL 3-Topping for only $11.99 from www.papajohns.com for lunch or dinner! Use Promo Code 121509") ("Papa John's Pizza"), or other events in order to show that they, like their customers, have some shared experiences.

Both Papa John's and Domino's have understood that in order to find success in social media, they need to let the way that the medium itself works do much of the selling for them. Advertising via social networking is not simply an online reproduction of traditional word-of-mouth advertising but rather a more complex process that functions according to Burke's theory of identification.

Social Politics

Kenneth Burke writes, "Identification ranges from the politician who, addressing an audience of farmers, says 'I was a farm boy myself,' through the mysteries of social status, to the mystic's devout identification with the source of all being" (xiv). While social media might not have much to offer in terms of a mystical experience, it does offer examples of politicians identifying with audiences and of public exhibitions of social status. In the 2010 U.S. midterm election, for example, the Pew Internet and American Life Project reported that 22% of adults who were online used Facebook or Twitter for political purposes to do things like discover who friends voted for, get information about a candidate, join or follow a political campaign or group, or follow election results in real time. The year 2010 also saw a much more equitable usage of social networking across political parties and age groups than was seen in 2008. Social media as a whole were on the rise in 2010, as 26% of all Americans used their cell phones for political purposes (Smith, "The Internet and Campaign 2010").

While not all candidates used social media effectively in 2010, those who did followed models similar to those used to garner business success for companies like Domino's or Papa John's. That is, campaigns that used social media to grow or maintain interest in their candidates did so by facilitating a sense of identification between themselves and those potential voters in their network. The Kentucky senate race between Rand Paul and Jack Conway was an instructive example. Paul's Facebook site featured photographic and video content showing Paul in both professional and personal moments. Not only did Paul's site offer information about the candidate and his platform (Web sites have done this for candidates since the mid-1990s), but it also showcased aspects of Paul's life that made his politics seem more personal. By contrast, Conway's Facebook site, though it had more pictures, had a minimal amount of content not related directly to his campaign. As PRNewsChannel.com reported on the day of the election:

> Rand Paul's Facebook page had 84,000 fans and shows videos, pictures of him trick-or-treating with his kids and talking with constituents. His Twitter page has 8,700 followers, even after he switched to a new username. His opponent Jack Conway only had 9,000 Facebook fans and 2,500 Twitter followers, but he updated several times throughout the day. His postings consisted of pleas for votes, reminders to tell others to vote and updates on issues from the campaign trail. Polls show Paul winning by double digits. Rasmussen had him up by 12 and Real Clear Politics showed Paul up by an average of 11 points. ("How Social Media")

This is not to suggest that candidates in 2010 won because they used social media well. In fact, there was no strong correlation between "likes" on Facebook (or other measures of social media success) and election results (Carr). ABC News reported that

> Delaware's Christine O'Donnell . . . had more Facebook and Twitter fans than Democrat Chris Coons did . . . but she lost resoundingly, by nearly 17 percent. . . . In the California Governor Race, Meg Whitman had more Facebook followers, but still

lost the race. Whitman had the third largest number of Facebook followers out of all candidates in 2010 . . . Republican Sharron Angle of Nevada, who raised more money from donors than any other Senate candidate, also was not elected. Angle also had more Facebook "likes" than Senate Majority Leader Harry Reid, but still could not win the election. (Schlesinger)

So while social media use didn't always translate to the polls, those candidates who used the technologies well and garnered the biggest followings were those who were able connect with their constituents most directly, share updates on campaign news and personal insight, and generally embrace the power of the technology to at least appear to be relatable and accessible. And though social media are just one type of communicative strategy used by a campaign, their significance in close elections, especially when they function to generate income for a campaign, is not easily dismissed.

Ultimately then, even though identification practices might provoke similar results in social media as they do in more traditional political contexts, their execution is somewhat different. That is, social media require that candidates become more open about those categories of their life that are deemed relevant by voters and by the organizing principles of the sites they use. Their success in approaching consubstantiality has much to do with their command of the expectations of both the audience and those virtual spaces in which they meet them.

Social Networking and Constitutive Rhetoric

While Burke's theory of consubstantiality might tell us something about how rhetorical identification works in social media, we need to look elsewhere in the rhetorical canon to make sense of the greater impact of social media on cultural norms and expectations. That is, social media are rhetorically significant not only because of the ways in which they connect people to one another discursively but also because of their greater cultural role as a form of self-expression. As is evidenced by some of the scholarship above, many of those who study social media are intrigued by the ways in which technology is facilitating a change in how we construct, present, and understand our identity. The question of how identity is constituted has been central to rhetorical theory for at least thirty years, and one central theme in that scholarship has been the explanation of identity as offered by Maurice Charland, who posits that rhetoric offers the potential to call someone into the performance of an identity.

The last sentence in Maurice Charland's 1987 essay on constitutive rhetoric suggests that rhetorical criticism can help demonstrate the ways in which "the position one embodies as a subject is a rhetorical effect" (148). In reading the rhetoric of the Quebec independence movement, Charland explains how a large percentage of the population of Quebec came to understand themselves as *Québécois*, a common people with a tradition, history, and set of life skills that necessitated a political fight for succession from Canada. Charland's project interrogates rhetorics (e.g., *The White Paper*) that were constructed for, deployed in, and taken up by a general public.

In the essay, he confronts a situation where the "identity of the audience is clearly problematic" (134). Charland's essay reads the White Paper, a document intended to explain the reasons for Quebec's independence from Canada, as a constitutive rhetoric.[3] His essay argues that this text does constitutive work because it assumes subjects who are

> in Althusser's language, "interpellated"[4] as political subjects through a process of identification in rhetorical narratives that "always already" presume the constitution of subjects. From this perspective, a subject is not "persuaded" to support [Quebec's] sovereignty. Support for sovereignty is inherent to the subject position addressed by the *souverainaiste* (pro-sovereignty) rhetoric because of what we will see to be a series of narrative ideological effects (134). . . . Interpolation occurs at every moment one enters into a rhetorical situation, that is, as soon as an individual recognizes being addressed. An interpolated subject participates in the discourse that addresses him . . . one must already be an interpolated subject and exist as a discursive position in order to be part of the audience of a rhetorical situation in which persuasion could occur. (140)

In constitutive rhetoric this recognition of an addressed subjectivity, interpellation must occur prior to the narrative: it is necessary to place someone in the position of wanting to hear a story before it can be successfully told. There must be an "inviting" of the reader to engage a text.

Key to Charland's analysis is the description of how the text is taken up by the people of Quebec. He claims that the White Paper becomes the basis for an embodied ideology, a form of daily practice that relies on the text to shape certain aspects of both public and private identity. In addition, he explains that constitutive rhetorics are also material because they are always oriented toward action. Even more important, Charland argues that the White Paper uses rhetoric to create a new subject position, one that has no material existence a priori the text. In other words, it provides a set of narratives that produce certain ideological effects: the subject becomes both historically situated and transhistorical, and, most important, the subject has an illusion of freedom (139–41). Charland explains that constitutive rhetorics can both "rework or transform subjects" and that "collective identities . . . in general only exist through an ideological discourse that constitutes them" (139).

The Internet has often been cited as a type of global village; it is considered to be a place where much of the world can meet to exchange ideas and information, do business, or share a laugh. The idea that someone can assume a new identity and become a new and "virtual person" online is also a frequent theme in both popular and scholarly commentary on the cultural impact of the Internet. Essentially, the Web provides a place where one can join niche communities; it is a space where an individual can find a "virtual home" to discuss hobbies, interests, fetishes, politics, and more.[5] In other words, the Internet has provided a meeting place for many subcultures and countercultures. However, the act of assuming an "online identity" presupposes that this identity is somehow meant to be divorced from the subject's day-to-day non-Internet communication. The argument here is that identity formation online is not as totalizing an experience as identity formation offline, in the real world. Charland's *peuple québécois* lived their lives differently and took political action as the result of a constitutive identity. Most people who join an Internet discussion group under the guise that they are someone other than who they "really" are do not usually change their normal, material practices in such drastic ways. A text can *only* be "constitutive" when it is able to make sense *within* a community's already existing perception of the potential of its own discourse.

What Charland's perspective on constitutive rhetoric allows us to do is to think about identity in social media from a metaperspective. That is, instead of focusing on the ways in which users can create certain kinds of identities for themselves by using the tools of the medium (as we did in chapter 2), we can instead consider how users' identity *as* social media users is determined in specific ways by the "text"—a social-networking technology or Web site—that enables and constrains the ways in which they think of their identity.[6] A constitutive theory of identity goes beyond an analysis of those categories of identification provided on the site (i.e., age, sex, gender, relationship status, or favorite band), but instead considers the ways in which participation in the site itself is a significant marker of cultural identity, shifting how we understand subjectivity more widely.

Studying Social Media: Further Considerations for Rhetoricians

While theories of consubstantial identification and constitutive rhetoric can help us understand something about the rhetorical functions of social media, these two approaches do not exhaust the potential for rhetorical criticism to address social media. We will end this chapter by briefly touching on some other existing concepts from the field that are potentially applicable to the study of social media. Though we do not have the space here to explore each idea to its fullest, it is our hope that the discussion can be an instigator of further research.

Apologia

It is well documented that much of Western culture is infatuated with celebrity and that the news media constantly stoke that interest by providing comprehensive coverage of celebrity court cases, scandals, romances, career shifts, and so forth. Increasingly, celebrities and their handlers have turned to Twitter as a way to promote their work, connect with their fans, and to stir publicity. As Twitter has grown in popularity, some of the biggest followings on the site belong to musicians, actors and actresses, prominent sports figures, and politicians; many have had to learn how to carefully manage their Twitter feed. Muntean and Petersen explain that:

> Hollywood has historically expended great energy and resources to perpetuate the myth that the star's image is univocal. In the present moment, however, studios' traditional methods for discursive control have faltered, such that celebrities have found it necessary to take matters into their own hands, using new media technologies, particularly Twitter, in an attempt to stabilize that most vital currency of their trade, their professional/public persona.

When these stabilizing actions go awry, it can result in undesirable news headlines. For example, following the death of terrorist Osama Bin Laden in May 2011, Pittsburgh Steeler Rashard Mendenhall used Twitter to chide people for celebrating Bin Laden's death by tweeting, "What kind of person celebrates death? It's amazing how people hate a man they never even heard speak. We've only heard one side" ("Mendenhall's Tweets"). Mendenhall's tweet earned him headlines on ESPN's Web site, discussion on sports television and radio shows, and exposure in the mainstream press outside of sports coverage. The comments (and other similar messages) prompted Steelers president Art Rooney II to issue an apology explaining that "it is hard to explain or even comprehend what he meant with his recent Twitter comments. The entire Steelers' organization is very proud of the job our military personnel have done" ("Mendenhall's Tweets"). Mendenhall himself was forced to pay a fine by the Steelers organization, and he created a blog to clarify his remarks and offer an apology (of sorts).[7]

Other examples of controversial celebrity tweets from early 2011 included Reggie Bush's comments about leaving his New Orleans Saints team (Yasinskas), tweets by comedian Gilbert Gottfried and rapper 50 Cent that poked fun at a devastating earthquake in Japan ("50 Cent"), and county music star Blake Shelton' homophobic remarks about gays (McDonnell). Not only do celebrities make social faux pas on Twitter, but they often use the medium to apologize for their online and offline actions. Shelton, for example, engaged in an apologetic dialogue with GLAAD via Twitter after his disparaging comments (McDonnell). Musician John Mayer opted for a Twitter apology following an uproar in February 2011 for his use of the N-word in a *Playboy* interview (Marikar).

The use of social media to issue formal and informal apologies, express regret, clarify misunderstandings, deny wrongdoing, or engage in other forms of apologia should be of growing critical interest to rhetoricians, who have a rich history of studying these kinds of acts. Susan Brinson and William Benoit, for example, have written extensively about the rhetoric of image repair and focused on actions and statements taken by companies and individuals who face public rebuke. More recently, Ryan Shepard and Kirsten Theye have written about political apologies issued during the Bush administration, and Emil Towner and Kevin Stein have studied apologies by the Dixie Chicks and Mel Gibson, respectively. How does an apologia function in online contexts where audiences are able to directly respond to those who are issuing mea culpas? Are there certain scenarios wherein an apology made in social media is itself sufficient or insufficient to meet an exigence? What is the proper protocol when social media accounts are compromised, such as was the case with Chrysler's official Twitter feed when an employee tweeted, "I find it ironic that Detroit is known as the motorcity and yet no one here knows how to fucking drive" ("Twitter Feed F-Word")? Must one apologize for something done under their name by another? There is yet much to pursue regarding the rhetoric of public apology in social media.

Agency

Though there seems to be consensus among many observers *that* social media are important for political engagement, it is not yet entirely clear *how* these media are important. This question becomes even more nebulous when considered from the perspective of activist (instead of electoral) politics: Can social media be a significant force in political change? What kinds of political and personal agency are promoted through the use of social-networking technologies?

In late 2010 and early 2011 some insight into the question of the political potential of social media was offered when activity on sites like Facebook and Twitter played an active role in the series of protests and regime changes in Northern Africa and the Middle East known as the "Arab Spring." In countries like Tunisia, Egypt, and Bahrain large groups of mostly young Arabs used social media to plan events, share news of what was going on during protests, gain global attention for their causes, and otherwise coordinate activities related to political action.

Furthermore, social-media sites sometimes afforded protestors with an outlet for getting around government restrictions on other forms of communication or censorship. They played a significant role in countries like Egypt, where social networking was used to alert the broader world of on-the-ground developments when cell phone calls were blocked or limited and state and local media were silent. In an interview with *60 Minutes*, Egyptian Google executive Wael Ghonim, one of the leaders of the protests, remarked, "Without Facebook, without Twitter, without Google, without YouTube, this would have never happened. . . . If there was no social networks it would have never been sparked" ("Social Media, Cellphone").

It is worth emphasizing that while the Arab Spring was not created by social media (it was a response to many years of repression and ongoing grassroots efforts to provoke rupture), the speed with which it was carried out across the region was undeniably due, in part, to the use of these new media. Whether that remains significant in the future is still undetermined, for as Evgeny Morozov wrote for the *Guardian*:

> Today, the role of the telegraph in the 1917 Bolshevik revolution—just like the role of the tape-recorder in the 1979 Iranian revolution and of the fax machine in the 1989 revolutions—is of interest to a handful of academics and virtually no one else. The fetishism of technology is at its strongest immediately after a revolution but tends to subside shortly afterward.

Malcom Gladwell, in a *New Yorker* piece titled "Does Egypt Need Twitter?" raised a related point when he explained that "people with a grievance will always find ways to communicate with each other. How they choose to do it is less interesting, in the end, than why they were driven to do it in the first place." Nonetheless, the question of how social media function in contemporary activist rhetoric is one that critics must consider if they are to understand connections between new media technology and human agency.

Narrative

One other feature of social media that bears some consideration from rhetoricians is the way in which users' actions in the technology tell a story.[8] That is, since most social-media sites allow users within a network to browse through the history of those they are connected to, temporality plays an important role in shaping any meaning audiences might take away from the sites. For example, a site like Linkedin can provide us with someone's career history, Facebook might inform us about their past relationships, photos shared on Flickr can let us know where people have visited and when, and Twitter comments can clue us in to a user's thoughts about world events or personal crises. As the quantity of an individual user's postings to these sites increases, so too does the amount of information needed to piece together a narrative about their life.

That said, because of the fragmentary character of most social network feeds, traditional methods of narrative analysis might not be productive for critics who are interested in how narrative meanings are communicated in these media. A common rhetorical approach would be like that offered by Foss, who suggests that

> narrative criticism involves two steps: (1) a comprehensive examination of the narrative; and (2) selection of elements on which to focus. The first step involves examining a narrative in detail to gain a comprehensive understanding of it as a whole. The second involves focusing on those aspects of the narrative that allow the critic to answer the research question that guides analysis. (402)

Foss proposes that step 1 be carried out through examination of setting, characters, narrator, events, temporal relations, causal relations, audience, and theme. Step 2 involves a selection of significant elements: "If the critic's interest is in the impact a narrative is likely to have on efforts to negotiate a peace treaty between two countries, the critic would use the significant features identified—perhaps the temporal and causal relation of the narrative—to suggest what the impact is likely to be" (405). Foss discusses the difficulty of separating the what (content) from the how (form) in narrative, and posits that the selection of these significant elements will provide insight into the "deeper" values at work in a text.

When examining social media, it is clear that many of the elements that Foss suggests that a critic should consider—such as temporal relations and themes—are much more difficult to understand when viewing someone's personal feed than they might be in traditional narrative prose. There can be long gaps and frequent disjuncture between posts, the content and the form are often tied together in unique ways (such as the character limit for a Twitter post), and the settings, characters, and events are almost always designed to be secondary to the narrator-protagonist (the person who is featured). The digital context also introduces hyperlinks, sharing, and other interactive features into the story that should be accounted for when considering a narrative's causal relations or audience. To better analyze narrative in light of some of these differences, a more nuanced theory of the rhetoric of narrative is needed.

Some of Paul Ricoeur's scholarship on narrative is specifically concerned with the relationship between temporality and narrative. Ricoeur suggests that every narrative combines two dimensions: chronological and nonchronological. The first (chronological) is the episodic dimension; the second (nonchronological) is the configurational dimension (174). The episodic dimension is "the linear representation of time" (174) that allows both the "adding" of events to a narrative as well as provides an order that coincides to "human and physical events" (175). The configurational dimension "makes the succession of events into significant wholes that are the correlate of a group acting together" (175). Repetition, claims Ricoeur, which is always present in the narrative mode, is the foundation for historiography. This is because history actively searches for patterns in the past that can be reflected in the present. For the study of social media, Ricoeur gives rhetoricians a way to think about how discreet events, which are how updates to social media are published, might function together in interesting ways to create meaningful narratives. Furthermore, social media facilitate collective authorship, suggesting that groups and collectives can create their own narratives collectively. In other words, a postmodern perspective on narratives as fragmented, referential, and multivocal discourses is useful for the study of how narratives unfold in social networking contexts.

Conclusion

Social media continue to be important to candidates and elected officials, and the role of sites like Twitter and Facebook in 2010 has prompted further efforts by both parties to enhance their presence in these and similar sites. It has also forced them to carefully consider their social media strategies moving forward toward 2012 and beyond. [9]As they do, critics of new media will need to do the same.

In this chapter, we have highlighted several ways in which rhetorical theory can be used to make sense of social media and social networking. Following a brief overview of research into social media, we discussed how a Burkean model of identification is productive for considering the actions of companies and candidates trying to reach audiences, how a theory of constitutive rhetoric is useful for thinking about how one's identity as a social media user is constructed, and we provided an overview of several additional concerns for rhetoricians interested in studying these sites and their users. In the next chapter, we look at another emerging kind of activity online: anti-institutional politics.

Notes

1. We are distinguishing between "social networking" as the name for an active process that one engages in and "social media" as those media (Web sites, smartphones, etc.) in which social networking can take place.
2. In 2007, for example, Facebook had only 20 million users. The year before, Andrew Chadwick wrote in the conclusion of his excellent *Internet Politics* that "'social software'…is only likely to augment online political activity" (325).

3. Charland explains that constitutive rhetoric "positions the reader towards political, social, and economic action in the material world" (141).

4. "Interpellation" refers to Louis Althusser's idea that "the process by which ideology addresses the (abstract) pre-ideological individual thus effectively producing him or her as subject proper . . . the situation always precedes the (individual or collective) subject, which precisely as subject is 'always-already interpellated'" ("Interpellation [philosophy]").

5. Our discussion of TeaPartyNation's Web site is an example of a site that functions, in part, through processes of interpellation.

6. We do not mean to suggest here a strict determinist view of new media (e.g., the Internet causes a specific kind of change). A constitutive rhetoric is about an invitation, a possibility, a "hailing" that when acknowledged has certain consequences for identity. Human agency still factors prominently in this kind of scenario.

7. Mendenhall explained that "nothing I said was meant to stir up controversy. It was my way to generate conversation. . . . I apologize for the timing as such a sensitive matter, but it was not meant to do harm" (R34Mendenhall).

8. For more on this, see chapter 1 for a discussion of Jamie Bianco's work on the growth of Facebook.

9. U.S. House Republicans, for example, have taken to annual contests to amass the highest amount of followers (Scola). Newt Gingrich has suggested that spending on social media in 2012 must be significant (Rodriguez).

7

Anti-Institutional Politics Online

Activism, Hacktivism, and Digital Confrontation

Much of our focus thus far has been on how new media technologies have been used to promote mainstream political candidates and causes. Our discussion of national and local elections, viral video, social networking, and other uses of the Web and related technologies has been squarely focused on what can be deemed "institutional politics." That is, we have focused on examples of how new media are either used by established political institutions or examples of political practices that are legally and culturally sanctioned. In this chapter, we shift the focus to "anti-institutional politics": unconventional, unsanctioned political practices aimed at challenging established institutional power structures.

In chapter 1 we briefly discussed Wikileaks as an example of a Web-based movement that functions as a kind of counterpublic. Wikileaks, however, is only one of the most recent examples of Web-based anti-institutional politics. In this chapter, we will consider several other examples from the recent history of the Web. Important to this discussion is a larger question of the place of anti-institutional politics in the contemporary political climate, where many forms of protest can be confined to free speech zones, denounced as unpatriotic, or prosecuted as terrorism. Does the Web offer a context in which these radical acts might be able to attain a degree of success without the legal and physical limits imposed on physical space? Are confrontational politics, when carried out in virtual networks, able to make a sufficient impact in the public sphere so as to provide a sustainable model of social movement?

We will begin by defining, discussing, and historicizing one particular kind of anti-institutional politics, hacktivism, as a form of protest that is tied to the long-standing tradition of English and American radicalism. Following this, we will consider how and why this form of anti-institutional activism has been frequently framed as "cyberterror" in public rhetoric by focusing on several recent cases. Finally, we draw on the work of Paul Virilio to make sense of the rhetorical tactics used by anti-institutional political movements in digital contexts, and we will set up some basic theoretical assumptions for examining similar protest activities.

Hacktivism as Anti-Institutional Politics

As hacking-related activity becomes more prominent in global politics, these questions are of growing significance. While there are some actions that are in clear violation of law (such as private phone hacking by the UK newspaper the *News of the World* or the theft of money from bank accounts through the use of stolen account details and online wire transfers), there are also an increasing number of hacking activities aimed at protesting institutions,[1] providing work-arounds to government firewalls,[2] or exposing security flaws in an effort to strengthen security.[3] These latter cases are known as hacktivism.

Hacktivism is perhaps most succinctly defined as politically motivated hacking, though this definition fails to account for the wide spectrum of digitally based protest activities that sometimes fall under the term "political." For example, in American media, hacktivism is often presented (by its targets and supporters alike) as activity that operates in direct confrontation to the U.S. government's democratic processes or diplomatic policies; hacktivism is "political" action that doesn't adhere to traditional American standards of deliberation such as voting, appeals to elected representatives, use of the courts, public marches, and so forth. As such, the ideologies that shape hacktivist action are usually understood by those in power as a primarily foreign threat. In her essay "Hacktivism: An Emerging Threat to Democracy," Dorothy Denning offers an illustration of these standard denouncements of hacktivism:

> In the wake of NATO's accidental bombing of China's Belgrade embassy in May 1999, angry Chinese allegedly hacked several U.S. government sites. The slogan "down with barbarians" was placed in Chinese on the home page of the U.S. embassy in Beijing, while the U.S. Department of Interior Web site showed images of the three journalists killed during the bombing, crowds protesting the attack in Beijing, and a fluttering Chinese flag. A Department of Energy Web page displayed the message "Protest U.S.A.'s Nazi Action!" ("Hacktivism")

As the title of her essay suggests, she views this type of action as detrimental to the resolution of political differences through democratic, dialogical processes. In addition, she argues that the fallout of this type of hacktivism is potentially harmful for U.S. diplomacy; the discourse is incendiary, and the actions "generate fear."

As we will see in this chapter, Denning's sentiment recurs across many statements made by the U.S. military in response to breaches of network security. There is, of course, absolutely no tolerance for these actions by the state that they are often targeting. Any and all forms of hacktivist protest are viewed as harmful to diplomacy, democracy, secrecy, military efficiency, and intelligence gathering. Perhaps more important, even though the hacking of U.S. government and military networks dates to the early days of computing, since the late 1990s (and especially after September 11, 2001) these actions have been refigured by the federal government and the U.S. military as a form of "cyberterrorism"—a moniker that increasingly places those who participate in legitimate forms of computer-based protest at personal risk. By equating hacktivist protest with other forms of terrorism through a series of strategic rhetorical moves, the government has been able to deal harshly with individuals and organizations that it catches engaging in the type of action described by Denning. This rhetorical shift has serious implications for the role of radical forms of dissenting politics (not only those protesting the military) within a culture that embraces technology in everyday life. In other words, what has been created is a rhetorical situation wherein both hacktivists and government agencies are placed on the defensive, limiting the potential for new types of dialogue offered by Internet technologies.

Pushing against the popular dismissal of hacktivism as a form of terror, we propose instead that hacktivism is a recent and important development in a longstanding American and British tradition of radical political protest; specifically, it is an activist movement whose rhetoric draws on those radical protests that have taken place during national times of war. As such, it is often aggressive, antagonistic, and ingenious, though not necessarily terrorist. Framing hacktivism in this way is important because it allows us to trace the relationships between the conditions of emergence for hacktivist action (context), the ways in which hacktivist acts are carried out and subsequently addressed (processes of action and repression), and the implications that all of this has for shaping what it might mean to discuss contemporary activism, digital rhetorics, and the status of an emerging cybercitizenship.[4]

Antagonism and Invention: The History and Theory of Radical Resistance

While public protest against any type of institutional authority can take on many forms, history suggests that those protests aimed at the military in particular have been some of the most innovative and creative. Mass demonstrations such as marches, sit-ins, or antiwar concerts have been familiar faces of antiwar protest in the latter half of twentieth-century American politics. Traditional forms of war protest also have included workers' strikes, filibustering, and various peaceful forms of consciousness raising. These forms of protest are largely accepted (by the state and by the public) to be legitimate forms of war resistance within a democratic nation that claims to protect free speech. In other words, while the government and military may not like war protest, they grant a certain freedom to speak out against the war providing that demonstrators remain peaceful and obey the law.[5] Though occasionally these forms of protest result in violence by the state against the protesters (and vice versa), violent actions are often explained away as the unfortunate but inevitable result of deviation from acceptable forms of political protest.

As Tarrow puts it, states that choose policies of tolerance for protest movement (instead of policies of repression) create a "double-edged sword" for those involved in the protest. That is, governments that are tolerant do provide a freedom of assembly and foster "a sense that [the participants] are acting meaningfully on behalf of their beliefs," but, at the same time, they "deprive organizers of the potent weapon of outrage" (84). Some groups are then forced to posit their unrecognized arguments into nonsanctioned spaces of protest or into unconventional activities— including but not limited to violence. It is in these gray areas that radicalism is born.

This chapter is interested in the forms of protest that do not obey the law and that do not necessarily remain peaceful. There is a rich tradition of political forms of protest against military action that might be deemed "radical politics." The term "radical politics" itself is rooted in a tradition of British radicalism that can be traced back at least to the mid-seventeenth century. This history is reflected in R. J. White's introductory remarks to his pamphlet *Radicalism and Its Results 1760–1837* that demonstrates the complexity of the term:

> Radicalism with a large "R," unlike Conservatism with a large "C" and Liberalism with a large "L," is not a historical term of even proximate precision. There was a never a Radical Party with a national organization, local associations, or a treasury. But there were, and there are "Radicals"…although the breed may be a genus containing species, the individual is the proper object to be studied. (3)

White's comment points to one of the difficulties critics of social movements face when they examine radicalism: radical movements are often more individualistic, less organized enterprises than more traditional forms of social movement. In the time referenced here, there was no formal radical party; instead the British Parliament contained non-party-affiliated MPs who were especially outspoken on specific issues and thus considered to be radical.[6] As we shall see, this spirit of individualism is an important and defining component to the British and American tradition of political radicalism. When examining historical instances of radical action in either of these countries, it is often the case that individuals act alone on behalf of a radical belief as opposed to functioning as a participant in an organized protest or as a member of a political party.

"Radicalism" as a term, then, has historically meant very different things to different people. In eighteenth-century France, for example, the term had connotations of revolution that were not as relevant to conceptions of radicalism in early nineteenth-century England. Neither of the uses of these terms fully explains the socialist (and especially communist) connotations that the term took on in early twentieth-century American politics. And while we will trace the spatial and temporal nuances of this term below, it seems important to make some initial (though very general) claims about how radicalism is being understood for the scope of this chapter. Specifically, there are three definitional components to radicalism: circumvention, antagonism, and invention.

First, it is important to distinguish radicalism from other political "isms" like socialism or anarchism. Radicalism does not push for the dissolution of a state as such, but for particular changes to the current state (usually through either revolution or reform). Sidney Tarrow talks about radicalism as part of the cycle of both revolutionary and nonrevolutionary movements. He ties radicalism to repression and notes that "where [government] repression is unfocused, inconsistent and arbitrary, or where it is limited by international or domestic pressures" the movement becomes more radical. In addition, he explains that this "radicalization also depends on internal relations in the opposition" (158). In other words, radical politics is appealing because it exploits weaknesses in institutional structures of control and, as such, often succeeds in accomplishing its political objectives. Radical political protest, then, can be understood as that which forgoes conventional or official appellate systems and circumvents traditional democratic avenues of reform (such as elections or congressional hearings).

Second, radical movements draw on a spirit of antagonism, which can be understood as a frequently hostile, impassioned response that results from tensions between conflicting and disparate politics, ethics or ideologies. From a radical perspective, structural solutions to address grievances are either inadequate or do not exist at all.

Laclau and Mouffe discuss antagonism as a condition that is born out of the impossibility of stable and situate antagonistic action at the limit of political engagement because it is literally the point at which the limit of the social has been reached; "antagonisms are not *internal* but *external* to society...[they represent society's] impossibility of fully constituting itself" (125). While the forms that antagonisms take are grounded in specific conditions of emergence, the antagonist impulse appears as the result of a frustration with social order. In an initially confusing passage, they explain:

> The limit of the social must be given within the social itself as something subverting it, destroying its ambition to constitute a full presence. Society never manages fully to be society, because everything in it is penetrated by its limits, which prevent it from constituting itself as an objective reality. We must now consider the way in which this subversion is discursively constructed. As we have seen, this will require us to determine the forms assumed by the presence of the antagonistic as such. (127)

In other words, antagonism is that process of subversion that stops society and the institutionalized forces that shape everyday experiences from achieving permanence; antagonism keeps things fluctuating, uneasy. Important, the antagonistic is always discursively constructed; as such, the forms antagonistic rhetorics take can only be understood in relation to a rhetorical exigency.

It is because of this ongoing struggle between a stable social and the destructive limit that the third component of radicalism emerges: an emphasis on invention. As antagonistic rhetorics need to adapt to new discursive forms, it is the function of processes of rhetorical invention to delineate these methods of subversion.[7] Often, these methods of subversion can situate in or be carried out through the use of new technologies.[8] Historically, radicals have turned to various technical innovations to achieve their political goals (seventeenth-century English Papists used gunpowder and spread pamphlets, Luddites used old technology to break new machines, American World War I pacifists focused their energies on key industrial and transportation sites, and American GIs during World War II used cheap printing technology to their benefit, etc.). This inventional dimension to radical politics is also found in hacktivism.

The importance of invention to political success—radical or otherwise—is something that rhetorical scholars have long noticed. Aristotle wrote that "it is evident that it is first necessary…to have selected statements about what is possible and most suited to the subject" (Kennedy, 188). Invention was included as one of Cicero's five canons of oratory; he writes in *De inventione* that it is "the conceiving of topics either true or probable, which may make one's cause appear probable." The importance of invention for social movements extends past the creation and selection of arguments to the determination of exactly how these arguments will be voiced; invention becomes the driving force of innovation. Tarrow explains that movements have learned to respond to shifts in institutional tactics by shifting their own strategies. He cites a number of activities such as using computerized mailing lists, seeking celebrity endorsements, increasing professionalization, and creating television advertising as basic examples of how social movements innovated in the twentieth century. None of these innovations is necessarily radical, though. They are responses to both state measures of control and shifting patterns in audience behaviors, but they do not in and of themselves fit the definition of radicalism that we are working with here ("that which forgoes conventional or official appellate systems and circumvents traditional democratic avenues of reform").

Drawing on an Aristotelian concept from *The Nicomachean Ethics*, Kevin DeLuca writes that the concept of phronesis (and its emphasis on the particular) is relevant when considering why specific social movements use specific tactics (44). Phronesis is "'the intelligent understanding of contingency' [Charland] that guides praxis in an open social field" (44). This type of action requires a social movement to "seize on the wing the possibilities that offer themselves at a given movement" (76) and create tactics that will work in a particular context. In a digital context, "seizing on the wing of possibilities" means taking full advantage of what is made possible through technology.

Hacking as Protest: Radicalism in the Information Age

In the United States especially, the military remains at the cutting edge of technology development and networking security. Additionally, the military has a long history of engaging in data gathering and creating "secured" data storage. These types of actions conflict with the ideals suggested by the hacker ethic that champions a world in which information is free and accessible for all. That the military's use of technology is often associated with acts of aggression, controversial politics, and death and destruction increases its profile as a target for hacktivism.

There is a significant history—almost fifty years' worth—of hackers targeting military computers. Ironically, then, hacktivism is a form of protest that exploits the very technologies that the military uses to conduct its actions. Collectively, these examples and others like them suggest that there is no "standard" hacktivism attack formula. In some of the examples, attacks seemed to be based internationally and carried out by citizens of other nations; in others the attacks originate from within the United States. While the targets are all branches of the military industrial complex, the motives for the attacks are not always clearly linked to military actions in each instance (e.g., a particular war).

Over the next several pages we discuss four historical examples of hackers engaging the military to either break into systems and free information or to protest certain military actions that are indicative of this longstanding confrontation.

1. 1990–1991 Attack on DOD computers: An attack by hackers on the Department of Defense computer infrastructure (at thirty-four military installations) was carried out in 1990–1991. Jack Brock, of the Government Information and Financial Management Information Management and Technology Division, released this explanation of the activity in November 1991.

> At many of the sites, the hackers had access to unclassified, sensitive information on such topics as (1) military personnel—personnel performance reports, travel information, and personnel reductions; (2) logistics—descriptions of the type and quantity of equipment being moved; and (3) weapons systems development data. Although such information is unclassified, it can be highly sensitive, particularly during times of international conflict. For example, information from at least one system, which was successfully penetrated at several sites, directly supported Operation Desert Storm/Shield. (n.p.)

The hackers in question were discovered to be Dutch, and Brock's report ends with concerns about the international risk posed by weaknesses in government computer security: "These weaknesses will continue to exist and be exploited, thus undermining the integrity and confidentiality of government information."

It is difficult to classify this incident as hacktivism instead of outright hacking (or, properly, cracking), if only because the term "hacktivism" and its associated activities wouldn't be coined until at least seven years later. Although similar actions would be carried out by later hacktivists (with the stated goal of interfering with the military), this particular case is more consistent with the type of military hacking that had historically taken place in the 1980s, the earliest days of hacking: the goal is to liberate information. In the aftermath of this particular incident, there was no evidence that the hackers had done anything with the information they had collected except to store it. In addition, though investigators searched for ties between the Dutch hackers and other government intelligence agencies, none was found.

2. August and September 1996 defacements of Department of Justice and CIA homepage: Two examples of hacking the government that are nearer to the aims of many contemporary hacktivism groups can be found in the alterations made to major government Web sites in August and September 1996. In August the main page of www.doj.gov, which belongs to the Department of Justice, was changed so that the page featured Adolf Hitler's picture instead of the attorney general's and was titled the "Department of Injustice" (this site is stored at http://www.2600.com/hacked-philes/). The site also included a list of top pornography Web sites whose most frequent visitors could be traced to ".gov" domains. The hackers posted an explanation for the defacement: the changes were made to protest government regulation of the Internet. These charges were expressly stated on the hacked site:

> Free speech in the land of the free? Arms in the home of the brave? Privacy in a state of wiretaps and government intrusion? Unreasonable searches? We are a little behind

our 1984 deadline, but working slowly one amendment at a time. It is hard to trick hundreds of millions of people out of their freedoms, but we should be complete within a decade. ("CIA Hacked")

The site was down for several days before being fixed. Shortly after it was repaired, the CIA Web site was attacked. Their standard homepage was replaced with a greeting welcoming visitors to the "Central Stupidity Agency." A CNN report explains the details:

> A person or group calling themselves "Power Through Resistance" created the hacked page which included obscenities and several links to various Internet sites, including Playboy, Hackerz.org, Flashback Magazine and protocols from The Swedish Hackers Association. A picture of an unknown man replaced that of CIA Director John Deutch. There was also an attack on an attorney named Bo Skarinder, who was urged to "Stop Lying." ("CNN—Hacked CIA Web Site")

The CIA site was also down for several days before being fixed. Responses by DOJ and CIA officials to these actions were banal and clichéd; they claimed to not understand the motives behind the attacks nor who had launched them.

3. 2001 Defacement of Departments of Labor and Health and Human Services Web sites by Chinese hackers: The *Pittsburgh Post-Gazette* reported in April 2001 that another in a series of competing attacks on government Web sites between warring hacking groups had taken place:

> Sites operated by the departments of Labor and Health and Human Services were working properly yesterday after being vandalized one day before by hackers believed to be from China. A picture of Wang Wei, the Chinese pilot who was killed in a collision with a U.S. Navy spy plane April 1, was posted Saturday on Labor's Web site. Technicians soon had the site fixed. The surgeon general's site was disabled entirely. HHS technicians added extra protections to the site's Web pages before putting them back online again. ("U.S. Web Sites Hacked, Fixed.")

Here, the focus of the attack was not so much on the military as on the U.S. government as a whole. However, it shares a number of features with the attacks listed above: the playfulness of the doctored pages, the action's origin outside national borders, and the initial difficulty of working around the hack by those in the government. Perhaps more significant than the target of the hack (the government) is the fact that the hack was part of an international hacker battle that had been initiated in response to military activity. This was confirmed in a *New York Times* report a month later when the battle had ended:

[Chinese] hackers, engaged in a "cyberwar" with their American counterparts, boasted today in a statement on a Chinese portal, Chinabyte, that they had defaced 1,000 United States Web sites in recent days, but had called a truce. American hackers mounted attacks on April 1 after a collision of a Navy surveillance plane and a Chinese fighter. Later, the Honker Union of China, an informal network, said it would start a blitz on May 1. At least six high-profile United States sites were defaced, apparently by Chinese hackers. ("Chinese Hackers Invade 2 Official U.S. Web Sites")

4. 2002 Arrest of Gary McKinnon for entering NASA and U.S. Navy, Army, Air Force, and Pentagon systems: McKinnon's case was a curious one. His actions were certainly geared toward the freeing of classified information, a recurrent theme in radicalism, but the information he sought on sci-fi concepts such as UFOs and antigravity technology initially appears to be highly apolitical. What his search succeeded in doing, though, was to investigate the military's digital infrastructure at one especially sensitive location: weapons development.

McKinnon explained that the reason he was trying to find information on "secret technologies" was to free information that he felt could improve the human condition. In this way, his motives were consistent with those informing many forms of hacktivist politics. In an article for masternewmedia.org, Robin Good discusses McKinnon's comments in a BBC interview:

> What McKinnon claims is that within the documents and records he has been able to access there is plenty [of] proof that the use of anti-gravity principles has been taken advantage of on this planet by yet unidentified groups....McKinnon claims to have been working on a "humanistic" agenda, with his efforts trying to verify how much of the claims made by a large group of scientists in respect to UFOs and anti-gravity technology were indeed being made inaccessible to the public at large....He was also interested in the positive aspects that would have resulted for humanity as a whole if this technology were to become available for everyone on the planet.

What was especially interesting about McKinnon's case was the response by the government. Before the enforcement of the USA Patriot Act, Phil Hirschkorn reported that McKinnon "faces a maximum penalty of five years in federal prison and a $250,000 fine for the New Jersey charges." A bbc.com article from June 2005, after the act went into full effect, illustrates the drastic difference three years makes: "Mr. McKinnon's solicitor, Karen Todner, estimates he could face a maximum 70-year jail sentence if convicted in the US" ("Military 'Hacker' Freed on Bail").

What do these four examples tell us about how hacktivists confront the military? For one thing, they suggest that there is no "standard" hacktivism attack formula. In some of the examples, defacement occurred while in others there are only instances of data theft. In some of the examples, attacks seemed to be based internationally and carried out by citizens of other nations; in others the attacks originate from within the United States. While each of the four attacks targeted part of the military industrial complex, the motives for the attacks were not clearly linked to military actions in each instance (e.g., a particular war).

What these examples do have in common, however, is more important than where they diverge. In each example, the attacks provoked some sort of official government response. It is these responses that are particularly interesting for the rhetorician: they explain how hacktivist protest has been taken up in official discourses. Specifically, these types of attacks proved to be the justification for a series of laws regulating the use of the Internet for activism. It is interesting that, though the examples above target government institutions, the legislation that follows these attacks increasingly protects corporate interests, private individuals, and some types of political speech (and not others). The next section of this chapter turns toward specific government initiatives aimed to curb hacktivism. As will become clear, there are certain aspects of digital rhetoric that make it possible for the government to restrict antagonistic protest grounded in information technologies.

The Rhetorical Construction of "Cyberterror"

Based on the examples in the previous section, over the past twenty years government responses to hacktivism targeting the military have become increasingly indignant and prosecution of those responsible has become a bigger priority.

It is also worth mentioning two government documents that are concurrent with the latter events in this timeline. The first, a 1997 report issued by a commission on computer crime to the Clinton White House, is notable because of its influence in shaping early government policy for defining and dealing with "computer crime"; it makes several assumptions:

> The number of unauthorized intrusions will continue to grow, owing to a steady increase in the numbers of people with capability and the increased availability of intrusion tools....Even assuming perfect reporting of intrusion incidents, law enforcement will not be...able to provide a sufficiently robust response to achieve maximum deterrence....Additional deterrence will be needed to thwart a growing threat. ("Approaches to Cyber Intrusion Response")

This report and its proposals for how to deal with this situation can be seen as resulting in Clinton's installation of the Cyber Corps program in 1999. The program was put into place to combat what had begun to be called "cyberterrorism." Clinton remarked:

> Open borders and revolutions in technology have spread the message and the gifts of freedom, but have also given new opportunities to freedom's enemies....We must be ready—ready if our adversaries try to use computers to disable power grids, banking, communications and transportation networks, police, fire, and health services—or military assets. (Goodin)

The late 1990s, then, mark a shift in the federal government's responses to digital transgressions against government and military institutions. Aside from the institution of specific laws aimed at criminalizing and fighting the types of computer-based attacks that had become increasingly common, there is a marked shift in the rhetoric of classification: hackers, crackers, hacktivists and others (script-kiddies,[9] warez d00dz,[10] etc.) could all be labeled under the wide banner of "cyberterrorist."

In other words, prior to this legislation, the legal meaning of terms like "cyberterrorist" and "cyberterrorism" was just as open to negotiation as the terms "hacker" or "hacktivist." In "The Myth of Cyberterrorism," Joshua Green explains his perspective on the term: "Cyberterrorism" merges two spheres—terrorism and technology—that most lawmakers and senior administration officials don't fully understand and therefore tend to fear, making them likelier to accede to any measure, if only out of self-preservation." Denning, on the other hand, is more exacting in her definition:

> Cyberterrorism is the convergence of cyberspace and terrorism. It refers to unlawful attacks and threats of attacks against computers, networks and the information stored therein when done to intimidate or coerce a government or its people in furtherance of political or social objectives. Further, to qualify as cyberterrorism, an attack should result in violence against persons or property, or at least cause enough harm to generate fear. Attacks that lead to death or bodily injury, explosions, or severe economic loss would be examples. Serious attacks against critical infrastructures could be acts of cyberterrorism, depending on their impact. Attacks that disrupt nonessential services or that are mainly a costly nuisance would not.

The legislation clearly sympathizes with this definition: the Clinton report even references Denning's work in the bibliography.

Unsurprisingly, this term has increased in use during recent years, concurrent with the Bush administration's Global War on Terror. The USA PATRIOT Act includes a specific clause on cyberterrorism. There are a few clauses, all of which are ambiguous enough to result in prosecution for various forms of Web-based protest that are especially striking:

> [Cyberterrorism includes] damage affecting a computer system used by or for a government entity in furtherance of the administration of justice, national defense, or national security.

[Concerning prosecution for causing "loss"], the term 'loss' means *any reasonable cost to any victim*, including the cost of responding to an offense, conducting a damage assessment, and restoring the data, program, system, or information to its condition prior to the offense, and *any revenue lost, cost incurred, or other consequential damages incurred because of interruption of service.*

AMENDMENT OF SENTENCING GUIDELINES RELATING TO CERTAIN COMPUTER FRAUD AND ABUSE...any individual convicted of a violation of section...can be subjected to appropriate penalties, *without regard to any mandatory minimum term of imprisonment.* (USA PATRIOT Act, emphasis added)

The act calls for the training of law enforcement officers in combating cyberterrorism; it also has a number of clauses that encourage the seizure of personal computers should cyberterrorism be suspected. All of the hacking incidents listed above would fall under the actions outlined in the USA PATRIOT Act.

Furthermore, these policies have been bolstered by work done in programs such as the Comprehensive National Cyber Security Initiative,[11] which was put into place in 2008 by the Bush White House to monitor and protect federal networks, and the Obama administration's launch of USCYBERCOM in 2009,[12] a military program meant to tighten armed forces cyber-security and provide national cyber-defense on a day-to-day basis. Similar programs have launched in the United Kingdom, where clear instances of cyberterror have been discovered and perpetrators caught (such as Al Qaeda operative Younes Tsouli in 2007). And while the prosecution of clear-cut cases of threats to public safety and military infrastructure certainly must be seen as a positive, productive turn in official policy, the legal and popular ambiguity of the term "cyberterrorism" also has led to a myriad of other practices being labeled cyberterror, some of which might better be understood as hacktivism.

Three brief examples can help us understand how the label of "cyberterrorism" gets misapplied to actions that have nothing to do with nefarious breaches of national security.

The Hacking of Sarah Palin

Late in the 2008 presidential campaign a hacker used publicly available knowledge about Sarah Palin—such as her date of birth and high school mascot—to reset the password to her private Yahoo! e-mail account. Upon gaining access to the account, the hacker took screenshots of her inbox, several e-mails, personal photos, and her contact list and posted the info and images to the Web site 4chan.org and Wikileaks.org. The hack itself was fairly simple—Yahoo has a password recovery feature that allows any member to answer a series of questions in order to retrieve and reset their password. Many other services—from banks to online shopping sites—feature this same system for account recovery. For those whose personal lives aren't laid bare in the media and on the Web, this system works well. For high-profile political candidates, they are a dangerous proposition, and many such politicians are or should be dissuaded from using Web accounts.

In the days that followed, David Kernell, a twenty-year-old University of Tennessee student and son of Democratic State House Representative Mike Kernell, was indicted by a grand jury for charges of unlawful access to stored communications, intentionally accessing a computer without authorization across state lines, and fraud. The responses by the presidential campaigns were what you might expect—Danny Diaz, a spokesman for the Republican National Committee, said: "The fact that a Democratic activist—and possibly an Obama supporter—could go to these lengths is deeply disturbing and criminal." A McCain campaign spokesperson explained, "This is a shocking invasion of the governor's privacy and a violation of law. The matter has been turned over to the appropriate authorities and we hope that anyone in possession of these e-mails will destroy them." Obama campaign spokesman Bill Burton denounced the hacking as "outrageous" ("Governor Sarah Palin's Yahoo Account Hacked").

Since the arrest of Kernell happened so quickly, media quickly focused their attention on the self-proclaimed "Obamamaniac," who was characterized in his hometown papers as "standoffish" and a loner who was into computers and computer games. His high school history teacher explained, "He did the same kind of thing when he went to school here….He and another kid found a way to get onto the school's server—they just sat down and figured out the password" (Begley). Fox News' Bill O'Reilly called for those that hacked the account AND those that ran "despicable, slimy, scummy" Web sites that posted the images and thus "trafficked in stolen merchandise" to be sent to jail (Carlson). On the Web, many sites likened Kernell's actions directly to cyberterrorism (see cyberbullyingreport.com, cyber-terror-investigation.blogspot.com, etc.).

Overshadowed by the attention to Kernell were two other important outcomes from the Palin e-mail hack—outcomes that may have been less publicized but, perhaps, even more significant than the indictment of a Tennessee House member's son. First, soon after their system was exploited, Yahoo added an extra layer of security to their service that required users to register a separate e-mail account in order to make changes to or recover their passwords. Hacking, political or not, often exposes weaknesses in popular security techniques and—in some instances—the hacker does a kind of service to those companies who were otherwise unaware of the problems with their products. Second, the screenshots were leaked in the middle of the ongoing "troopergate" investigation surrounding Palin and indicated that the governor had indeed been using personal e-mail to conduct state business, a technique that allowed her to communicate through channels that could not be subpoenaed through open records laws. In other words, the hacking of Palin's e-mail account is an example of successful hacktivist action because it shed light on the governor's improper and potentially illegal usage of outside services to conduct official business.

The hacking of Palin's account represents an interesting and potentially trans-formational moment in the history of hacktivism. First, the high-profile nature of the target is currently the most well-known instance of politically motivated hack-ing. Thus, it was an opportunity to see how and if, in response to the act, hacktivism might be addressed by political parties and major news outlets. Their response— universal disdain for the act and swift judgment for the suspect—suggests that hack-tivism has done little over the years to position itself as a legitimate form of protest, despite successful actions against a wide variety of political targets.

Second, this event served as a potential opportunity for hacktivists themselves to publically defend their actions and argue for those rights to which they feel enti-tled. In other words, an ethical response to Kernell's arrest and the widespread con-demnation of the act in the press might have been a concerted effort by like-minded hacktivists to publically defend the hack, to publicize the strengths of the movement, or to define other forms of hacktivism as legitimate or not in and against this par-ticular hack.[13]

Kernell was eventually sentenced to a year and a day in prison; afterward Sarah Palin equated the incident to Watergate in a posting to Facebook:

> Violating the law, or simply invading someone's privacy for political gain, has long been repugnant to Americans' sense of fair play. As Watergate taught us, we rightfully reject illegally breaking into candidates' private communications for political intrigue in an attempt to derail an election. (Condon)

This kind of hyperbole is politically useful for candidates looking to appear tough on cyberterror but wrongfully equates radical hacktivism with attacks against the state. Also interesting is a more recent example that saw similar rhetoric used fol-lowing an attack on a corporate network.

The Hacking of the PlayStation Network

In April 2011, Sony's PlayStation Network (PSN) was attacked, seemingly, by a group of activist hackers[14] known as "Anonymous." Anonymous, whose previous targets included the Church of Scientology, Koch Industries, the Zimbabwe gov-ernment, and YouTube (among others), went after Sony for a number of potential reasons including (but not limited to) Sony's suit against hacker George Hotz (who broke Sony's encryption on their PlayStation 3 console) and the company's removal of the Linux operating system from the same console. The PSN attack resulted in the network being taken down for several weeks, the private details of customers being compromised, and Sony's stock taking a noticeable nosedive.

In a U.S. House hearing on the matter, Sony PlayStation head Kizuo Hirai explained that the action was one of "cyberterrorism," a sentiment also expressed by many of the users affected by the service. Typical of some of the comments found online are those by user n3td3v (who claims to be involved in counter-terrorism security) in response to a CNET story covering the hack:

> We in the counter-terrorism security community have really got to get past calling Anonymous a group or organisation, in the same way we need to stop calling al-Qaida the same thing. I've been monitoring the Anonymous situation and it appears they are following the same ways of al-Qaida, in that the 'decision making is centralised, but the execution of attacks is decentralised.' Anonymous seem to have the same strategy of al-Qaida in that pods of the ideology are spread out across the world in franchises. Anonymous aren't classed as a terrorist movement yet, but the principle of the ideology is very similar to that of terrorist movements such as al-Qaida. We've really got to keep an eye on this Anonymous stuff as it could morph into something a lot more serious in the future. (http://news.cnet.com/8301-27080_3-20059737-245.html)

Here we see the logic of the war on terror extended to actions that have previously been understood as criminal trespassing and data theft (at worst) or (at best) radical protest. Other examples across the Web echo the sentiments shared by the CNET user above. The long-running *Computer and Video Games* (CVG) publication explained on their Web site that "our very way of life has been attacked, and consciously acknowledged or not, we are reeling" and classified Anonymous as "a technological terrorist—one without the malevolence for bloodshed or tragedy, but a terrorist nonetheless. Our cosy [*sic*] reliance on Sony's steel walls has been splintered; our trust in the system spooked." CVG goes so far as to directly compare the attack on Sony to that made by Gary McKinnon on the U.S. military (both perpetrators were "hyper-intelligent and, no doubt, not exactly a darling of high society") (Ingham). A similar theme could also be found in comments made by Daniel Ray, editor in chief of CreditCards.com, who in an interview with FOX Business News borrowed war-on-terror language to suggest, "If we were still using the old color-coded terror alert, this would be the equivalent of going to "orange alert"—an attack on your bank account may not be certain, but there is a high risk and you should redouble your vigilance" ("Sony PlayStation Users").

In other words, in the case of the Sony network hack there is a public equating of an attack on a corporate server with an attack against a sovereign nation or innocent civilians. Even though no financial theft or other damages were reported by Sony's users, and even though the network breach was made possible in part by Sony's own lax security measures, the rhetoric surrounding the event and the hackers responsible was incendiary.

The Arrest of Wikileaks' Julian Assange

In chapter 1, we discussed Wikileaks and its release of records related to U.S. involvement in Afghanistan in 2010. From November to February of that year, the group grabbed international headlines once again by making public more than 250,000 diplomatic cables addressing a wide range of topics. According to the Wikileaks Web site:

> The cables, which date from 1966 up until the end of February this year, contain confidential communications between 274 embassies in countries throughout the world and the State Department in Washington DC. 15,652 of the cables are classified Secret....The cables show the extent of US spying on its allies and the UN; turning a blind eye to corruption and human rights abuse in "client states"; backroom deals with supposedly neutral countries; lobbying for US corporations; and the measures US diplomats take to advance those who have access to them. This document release reveals the contradictions between the US's public persona and what it says behind closed doors—and shows that if citizens in a democracy want their governments to reflect their wishes, they should ask to see what's going on behind the scenes. (Wikileaks)

Though these documents were obtained by people who submitted them to Wikileaks (and not through Wikileaks' own hacking), the public discussion about cyberpolitics and cyberterror was very similar to what has traditionally been associated with hacktivist activity. As these cables were released, international authorities began to search for Wikileaks' founder Julian Assange under a warrant for investigation of a possible sex crime, arresting him in London in December 2010. His actions and arrest sparked widespread commentary on the release of the information and on Wikileaks and Assange more generally.

Mitch McConnell, Senate Minority leader, spoke about Assange on NBC's *Meet the Press* and explained that "I think the man is a high-tech terrorist. He's done an enormous damage to our country" ("Meet the Press"). Sarah Palin went even further in a Facebook post, suggesting that Assange should treated like a member of al-Qaeda:

> Assange is not a "journalist," any more than the "editor" of al Qaeda's new English-language magazine *Inspire* is a "journalist." He is an anti-American operative with blood on his hands. His past posting of classified documents revealed the identity of more than

100 Afghan sources to the Taliban. Why was he not pursued with the same urgency we pursue al Qaeda and Taliban leaders?

Palin's Facebook posting and McConnell's televised retort of Assange punctuated a flurry of anti-Wikileaks discourse that permeated online news sources, talk radio, and other media outlets in the weeks surrounding his arrest.[15] However, their denouncing of Assange as a terrorist actually falls outside of a definition about what constitutes cyberterror given in a Senate Judiciary Hearing by Keith Lourdeau in 2004, when he was the deputy assistant director of the FBI's Cyber Division. Lourdeau explained that a cyberterrorist was:

> those individuals or groups that illegally access computer systems, spread malicious code, support terrorist or state sponsored computer operations, and steal trade secrets that present an economic and security threat to the U.S. ("FBI—Hearing on Cyber Terrorism")

The problem, in part, is that the definition of "cyberterror" does not fit the actions taken by Wikileaks and Assange since the group did not steal any of the information they circulated. Thus Wikileaks had successfully espoused a component of the "hacker ethic"—that information wants to be free—by publishing the information submitted to them (but taken by others).

Thus far, we have argued that digital forms of anti-institutional protest such as hacktivism should be considered a contemporary incarnation of radical protest. Specifically, we have emphasized where the discourses of both hacktivists and earlier radicals overlap; they frequently share political ideologies (e.g., varying degrees of anarchism, class-based struggles, disdain for oppressive institutions, especially the military), they both stress the use of innovative forms of activism, and they both circumvent traditional, institutionalized avenues for addressing social, political, economic, and personal grievances.

Furthermore, in examining institutional responses to radical protest, a pattern has emerged. Political radicals become refigured by the institutions they threaten as the physical embodiment of an invisible threat: Papists trials stressed the allegiance of the plotters to the devil; the Luddites were thought to be in political and economic allegiance with foreign governments that were antagonistic toward England; the Missourian pacifists were deemed traitors and persecuted accordingly, the editors of underground GI newspapers were investigated as potential Communist allies. And, as explained above, governments that were initially concerned that hackers posed an "external" threat, that they existed beyond our borders, have today classified hackers who engage in protests as "cyberterrorists," operating to harm the government, people, and corporations in the United States.

The next section of this chapter turns toward the question of why all computer-based attacks (whether political or criminal, whether taken against the government or against corporate or private interests) have been reframed as terrorism. We argue that the frequently circulated explanation that the Bush administration promoted "terrorist-centric" rhetoric in order to garner support for military actions fails to take into account both the actual historical context of the discursive shift (the late 1990s) and the important material differences between blowing up a building and defacing a Web site (the role of the digital). In order to understand why and how the U.S. government and military are able to take these strategic positions, we turn to the work of Paul Virilio.

Paul Virilio and the Aesthetics of Digital Protest

As indicated above, the history of radical politics suggests that radical protest is often denounced by the institutions being targeted; furthermore this denunciation usually implicates the radicals in conspiracy, sabotage, or collusion with other (ideological or political) enemies of that institution: devilish powers, Communists, terrorists, and so forth. In each instance, certain historical conditions must be in place already in order for the denunciation strategies to work: the church already must emphasize ongoing spiritual warfare; the military already must suspect Communist infiltrations in many aspects of daily life, and the government already must be actively engaged in suppressing terrorist acts. What, then, are the conditions of emergence for the denunciation of hacktivism as a form of cyberterrorism? Because this is a rhetorical shift that, backed by federal legislation, has strong implications for how Web protest might be carried out, on what preexisting discourses does this denunciation draw?

The answer to this question is not a simple one. There is not a singular event such as the DOD attacks in 1991 or the Web page hacks of 1996 that provides legitimacy to these claims that hacktivism should be equated with terrorism. Instead, the current policy on cyberterrorism emerges from three related places: the aesthetic features of the Web itself, the relationship of military technologies to Web-based protest, and correlative narratives about both computer hackers and terrorists in American popular and governmental culture. Understanding how policies of repression are formed helps us to recognize one more aspect of the digital landscape in which hacktivism takes place: it tells us both what features of hacktivism are seen as especially dangerous to the institutions being challenged as well as what risks might exist for those engaging in hacktivism.

In the examples above, the focus of protest is the military-industrial complex and the possibility for action is grounded in computer technologies. Therefore, Paul Virilio's writing about the relationships between the military, politics, and technology sheds light on the consequences that ensue when these three areas of discourse intersect.

Speed and Aesthetics

Much of Paul Virilio's work interrogates the relationship between technology and politics; he is especially interested in the increasing role of "speed" in both realms. In his analysis of the use of technology in the history of military conflict, Virilio explains how the increased speed of military technology leads to a distortion of physical space by time. In other words, militaries are invested in the project of collapsing space, of finding ways to secure and observe more space in less time. As military technologies transform into consumer technologies, this phenomenon becomes more widespread; no longer limited to the field of battle, technologies that emphasize speed begin to collapse and distort living spaces as well. Armitage's explanation is that as the "inventor of concepts such as 'dromology' (the 'science' of speed), Virilio is renowned for his declaration that the logic of acceleration is at the heart of the organization and transformation of the modern world." Virilio explains his interest in speed: "History progresses at the speed of its weapons systems" (*Speed and Politics*, 68).

As a consequence of this technology, he argues, human perception itself has become dictated by speed. In *War and Cinema*, he explains that in modern warfare the image of the battlefield is always in advance of the reality of actual battle; it exists on the screen, in satellite imagery, in "real-time" simulation. Because of these technologies, not only does the physical space of battle become colonized by time but also our very ways of looking at, and thus interpreting, the realities of physical battle change. This change in perception has material consequences. For example, in *Desert Screen*, Virilio remarks on the ability to engage in combat from remote locations via screens that relay satellite information; thus the truth of the war is not in having superior *vision* on the battlefield (which is necessarily slow and limited by human physiology) but in having superior information (which is fast and ever expanding). In this way, the field of perception changes from the horizontal to the vertical, from the realm of physical engagement to one of detached strategizing.

Virilio believes that the increased speed of weapons system development has resulted in a contemporary crisis of representation that bears heavily on the role and function of politics. This crisis of representation is necessarily historically situated; the existence of a "crisis" presupposes a prior moment of "non-crisis."

This crisis of representation, which many have labeled as a constituent feature of postmodernity, often plays out in contemporary aesthetics. Dick Hebdige (1979), borrowing from Lévi-Strauss, writes about the practical, political strategy of postmodernist, bricolage aesthetics. He explains that it is possible to critique the post-modern condition by mimicking it; namely, by mashing together disparate elements to create new effects. For him, as for Virilio, a postmodern aesthetic emphasizes the referential: of mediated pop culture, of the audience and of the aesthetic object itself.

The Web, as an aesthetic object, can be read as the embodiment of this crisis in representation. Speed dictates experience; interaction is "vertical" (in Virilio's sense of the term); its hyperlink structure invites the referential. Hubert Dreyfus writes:

> Web surfers embrace proliferating information as a contribution to a new form of life in which surprise and wonder are more important than meaning and usefulness. This approach appeals especially to those who like the idea of rejecting hierarchy and authority and don't have to worry about the practical problem of finding information. (12)

In *Lost Dimension*, Virilio discusses how computer-based technology reorients per-ceptions of space:

> With the screen interface of computers, television and teleconferences, the surface of inscription, hitherto devoid of depth, becomes a kind of "distance," a depth of field of a new kind of representation, a visibility without any face-to-face encounter in which the vis-à-vis of the ancient streets disappears and is erased. In this situation, a differ-ence of position blurs into fusion and confusion…distinctions of *here* and *there* no longer mean anything. (12–13)

The same features that make the Web appealing—its wealth of information, its pos-sibility for anonymity, its potential for connectivity—are the same things that also make it a potential threat to certain forms of institutional control. They are also the same things that lead to a distrust, suspicion, and fear of those who wield the tech-nology without fear, with expertise.

Digital aesthetics, then, are a threat because they operate at that limit of the social that Laclau and Mouffe discuss; it is here that antagonism originates. In the next chapter we will discuss this space more specifically, as it is the place from which argument is constructed. One feature of the digital, however, is especially impor-tant to Virilio: the chaotic structure of information technologies originates in the institutionalized, controlled structures of military research and development.

Military Technology Used Against the Military

The advent of the Internet doesn't necessarily change the rules or even the "form" of political activism; history suggests that the use of new technology frequently went hand in hand with political activism, revolution, and suppression. All sides in political conflict use the technology at their disposal: the Papists turned to gunpowder, the GIs to cheap forms of publishing, the hackers to tools developed for infiltrating other computers. This is the strength of invention, a necessary component to radicalism, as discussed earlier.

That stated, the use of Internet technology to conduct war protest is a particularly striking study in irony. Though it didn't receive the attention of other high-profile weapons programs, the Web was developed first and foremost for military use; defense grants funded much of the early academic research that led to the creation of the Web.[16] The reason that the military wanted this technology—to gain a strategic advantage in war—is indicated in Virilio's critique above. In a passage from *Pure War*, Virilio comments:

> Don't forget the Pentagon considers information a weapon…no one talks very much about the NSA and that's where the game is played out, the veritable revolution in military doctrine, wargaming [*sic*] with information, the ongoing game in the corridors of military power. (183)

Furthermore, the Web is a military technology that allows a certain disembodiment, a removal of the self from the field of combat. In another passage from *Desert Screen* he suggests:

> Man is no longer the centre of the world of anthropocentrism or geocentrism; he has become, in the course of the twentieth century, the end of the world of a scientific nihilism. The "man of war" is no longer a soldier but rather a thinker, he who invents and programs weapons of destruction. (138)

The military development of the Internet was (and, importantly, continues to be) a way to reduce the potential for physical confrontation: remote control warfare.

Thus, as far as the military is concerned, the great transgression of hacktivism is in using the technology for its intended purposes. Hacktivists tear apart the consumer-friendly version of Web technology and find ways to use it that are nearer its original intent: remote-controlled action. It is a safer form of activism, one that requires a certain expertise and allows for the possibility of the disembodied protester. Again from *Desert Screen*:

> Even if this latest stage of enslavement of man to the machine no longer exactly recapitulates that of the earlier voluntary servitude, the loss of the immediate contact induced by tele-technologies will lead to a similar social frustration. (132)

The hacktivist who engages the military is a curious animal: he or she turns to the very technologies that cause disillusionment to protest the institutions that produce those technologies.

Analogous Narratives

Emerging from the prior two sections is a binary of presence-absence. This binary is instructive for thinking about how hackers are thought of in relationship to the Web generally and to military protest specifically. In other words, hacktivists are both present (they engage in politics; they impede on [virtual] spaces; they leave a mark; they are discursive) and absent (they have no bodily presence; they function under anonymity; they move quickly). As Virilio notes, "All that counts is the speed of the moving body and the undetectability of its path" (*Speed and Politics*, 135).

This binary understanding of the hacktivist matches up neatly with popular discourse on terrorism; in fact it is the same binary that the government now uses to justify the "War on Terror." There are four analogous features in particular worth noting:

1. *Hackers, like terrorists, are hidden and must be found.* Furthermore, it is the role of the government to engage in this search by any means necessary. Both groups are excellent at covering their tracks, residing in difficult-to-access locations, and escaping after committing action.
2. *Hackers, like terrorists, move quickly and by surprise.* Part of what makes terrorism an act of "terror" is the sheer velocity and shock of the attack. Hacking is also action predicated on the use of the technologies of speed; it is often surprising.
3. *Hackers, like terrorists, don't follow the standard rules of engagement.* Terrorist organizations don't engage in traditional forms of warfare. Hacktivism circumvents institutional avenues for social redress.
4. *Hackers, like terrorists, are always in our midst.* Neither terrorists nor hackers exist as only a foreign, alien threat. Your neighbor may be either a terrorist or hacker. Vigilance is required of the citizen.

So what do these rhetorics tell us about the question posed above: What then are the conditions of emergence for the denunciation of hacktivism as a form of cyber-terrorism? Among other things, they give support to the argument that hacktivist protest stands as a form of radical political protest caught in the convergence of Web-based aesthetic representation, technology developed for military purposes, and an overlapping institutional figuration of the terrorist subject.

In protesting the military through innovative forms of resistance, hacktivists are not only implicated in the history of radicalism dating back to the seventeenth century (and thus subject to the same type of institutional denunciations) but also are participating in a form of protest that exploits the very technologies that the military uses to conduct actions. We have suggested here that this form of radicalism speaks directly to the postmodern political landscape—one that faces a crisis of representation. Furthermore, we have argued that Paul Virilio's work offers the critic the necessary lexicon and theoretical framework through which to rethink the relationship of the Web to both history and to contemporary politics.

Virilio's critique of military technologies emphasizes their facilitation of this representational crisis by adopting machines that turn combat into a vertical exercise. As these technologies enter into wider public use, they engage the representational crisis by emphasizing aesthetics of speed and disappearance. These are the features of digital radicalism that tell us something about what it might mean to discuss "digital rhetorics" more broadly.

A Rhetorical Theory of Digital Activism

What we have done in this chapter is to both sketch out the contexts in which the rhetorics of hacktivism operate as well as explain the ways in which these rhetorics generate certain types of uptake. In doing so, we have attempted to paint a picture of what it might mean to discuss hacktivist actions as a type of "digital radicalism." In addition, by drawing on Paul Virilio's work on the political and social impact of technology, we have tried to explain why the combination of hacktivism's historical conditions of emergence and contemporary discourses about terrorism have led to the institutional denouncement of any and all acts of hacking as "cyberterrorism."

In his book *Activism!* Tim Jordan explains that hacktivism is often action that fits into one of two (sometimes overlapping, necessarily contradictory) categories: (1) accessing and spreading censored or restricted information or (2) hijacking or blocking information in an effort to make a political statement. Both categories reflect the influence of what is known as the "hacker ethic," which stresses the individual's right to engage any and all information and technology for any political, scientific, technological, public, or personal reasons.[17]

Any tendency to immediately foreclose the possibility of linking hacktivism to "old" social movement theory should be resisted. In fact, hacking culture has more in common with traditional class struggles against economic and political institutions than with the "new" social movements' concerns about identity, recognition, and local action. Their noncollective, noninstrumental tactics emphasize not local but private information. One member of the Hacktivismo hacking group explains,

"We use aliases, we know how to keep ourselves secret." The importance of secrecy to hacktivism allows not only anonymity in group involvement but also the possibility for quick disappearance when confronted with police resistance. While there does seem to be a sense of community solidarity through collective action, there is little physical interaction with like-minded hacktivists or with the targets or beneficiaries of their actions. Hacktivists neither take to the streets for public demonstration nor do they search for individual recognition by institutions (including government, media, academia). The actions above indicate that hacktivism encompasses more than what Melucci explains as New Social Movements' emphasis on the "symbolic functions" of members in "hidden networks" (127) but is instead interested in "transgress[ing] the flows of information both to create new forms of protest and to generate a new, activist politics of information" (Jordan, 134).

How, then, might the rhetorical critic approach hacktivism? Hacktivism groups deliberately produce dense, arcane, and coded discourse. For example, much of the rhetoric of a group like Hacktivismo reflects a long tradition of using various forms of "leetspeak," a language that borrows many conventions from various forms of computer programming. Leetspeak revels in both obscure references and the ability of the individual using it to successfully generate or decode complex, "elite" discourses that demonstrate immersion in these subcultures. These strategies show how the aesthetic features of the Web that Virilio reflects on function to shape discursive practices.

Hacktivist discourses, such as the use of leetspeak or encrypted communications when addressing one another, help to justify the need for secrecy and the (often self-imposed) isolation of any individuals or groups engaged in hacktivist practice. In addition, usage of this language on official Web sites, in virtual chat rooms, and even in face-to-face conversation adds to feelings of solidarity against institutions (like the military) that promote information censorship.

More important, understanding the rhetoric of hacktivism as intentionally elusive and exclusive provides the rhetorical scholar with an opportunity to approach hacktivism as a form of activism that employs significantly different rhetorical tactics than those discussed in scholarship debating old or new activist movements. Furthermore, hacktivism is (dis/)organized through very different processes than those usually explained in old or new movement scholarship and is linked to other contemporary political movements through different channels than are traditionally used for group-to-group interactions.

In sum, there are three characteristics that suggest hacktivism offers a new model of activism—characteristics that can be understood as uniquely digital features of anti-institutional protest. First, participation in a hacktivism is not open to anyone; engaging in these activities requires a working knowledge of how to program, hack, or secure various information systems. Participation requires not only empathy with the cause but also the ability (not simply the desire) to work toward specific goals. Furthermore, becoming a member of a hacktivist group is something that can be done in secret, can require vastly different levels of personal involvement (in both time and resources), and will often result in no public recognition of success (or failure). Just like many social movements, hacktivism professes to be concerned with human rights (the right to information). But unlike many human rights movements, the strength and success of the protest action require selective, highly trained, and anonymous membership.

Second, hacktivism's tactical actions are often carried out with the speed and precision of smart missiles. When announcements are made, software is released, or public (Internet-based) protests occur, those who are responsible for the action quickly disappear or disguise their identities to escape police action. McKinnon's capture is more the exception than the rule. In this way, hacktivist action can't be completely dissociated from theories of terrorist violence, though their emphasis on the elimination of information security or censorship (as opposed to human life or material goods) is an important distinction that is often lost in the discourses surrounding "cyberterrorism." Specifically, unlike groups that search for "recognition of identity" or "symbolic victory" (as in new social movements) or "material redistribution" through prolonged protest against the "vulnerable state" (old social movements), most hacktivism is intended to circumvent democratic channels of persuasion and produce immediate, effectual changes (albeit sometimes through the use of strategies that emphasize the symbolic or the material). This is where the links between hacktivism and a history of radical protest are most clearly seen.

Finally, hacktivism's interaction with social movement organizations is decidedly unique. While finding it necessary to adapt discourse styles to work with other human-rights activist groups, computer scientists, or (rarely) the government and the press, hacktivism is decidedly oblique and inaccessible to the uninitiated. Because of this, hacktivism does not always fit neatly or work well as part of other causes—even those who are interested in fighting military oppression or information censorship.

These three characteristics—exclusiveness/elusiveness of membership, the speed of appearance/disappearance of their actions, and the difficulty of interacting with other groups—suggest that rhetorical analysis of digitally based activism must account for one key feature that is not currently considered: the rhetorics of obfuscation. Obfuscation rhetorics are used to cover one's tracks, to hide, to erase the trace of authorship and participation in activist activity, to make understanding difficult.[18]

This variable of obfuscation, or at least the level to which it is employed, is something new in the rhetorics of radical protest: the Papist conspirators were tried and killed for their transgressions that had been made public through a series of pamphlets; many of the Luddites who wrote inflammatory letters or held public meetings also engaged in physical combat with the British military; the Missouri pacifists faced widespread persecution and (at times) government sanction for their very public acts of defiance, and many Vietnam GIs faced court martial for publishing authored and signed content in underground newspapers. Most of the participants in these groups used their real names, found ways to engage a wide public, and understood there was a high personal risk engaging in radical politics, especially if the movement failed. While radical movements have always circumvented "accepted" forms of public redress, more often than not the chosen avenues resulted in an even more public form of protest.

Conclusion

In this chapter we discussed the place of anti-institutional political movements in the digital arena and in the larger public sphere. We tracked how hacktivism, a long-standing form of anti-institutional protest, has been utilized to challenge the restriction of information and to protest various agencies and organizations. We also discussed how these challenges have, over time, been classified as examples of cyberterrorism. In the latter half of the chapter we discussed the rhetorical significance of this classification and explained how digitality affords for a particular kind of dynamic between protestors and those being protested against. The questions addressed in this chapter continue to loom large in public deliberation about the future of global Internet politics. Actions taken by groups like Anonymous or Wikileaks are only the most recent in a long history of anti-institutional politics, and though their connection to new media technologies helps to define them, it also makes their legal and moral grounding more tenuous.

In the next chapter, we will turn to some final thoughts about this project as a whole.

Notes

1. For example, 2009 actions by Iranian hackers using Slowloris took down government sites. Wikipedia explains, "During the protests that erupted in the wake of the 2009 Iranian presidential election, Slowloris arose as a prominent tool used to DDoS [distributed denial of service attacks] sites run by the Iranian government. The belief was that using a traditional

style of DDoS would affect Internet access for the government and protesters equally, due to the significant bandwidth they can use. The Slowloris attack was chosen instead, because of its high impact and relatively low bandwidth. A number of government run sites were targeted during these attacks, including gerdab.ir, leader.ir, and president.ir" ("Slowloris").

2. An example would be a Web browser known as "Torpark" developed by the group Hacktivismo. Torpark "causes the IP address seen by the Web site to change every few minutes, to frustrate eavesdropping and mask the requesting source" (Broersma). This potentially allows people in countries with strict government monitoring to browse restricted sites without fear of being caught.

3. This is known as "ethical hacking" and is sometimes used by companies to test their own security.

4. In this context, the term "cybercitizen" is meant only to mean someone who uses Internet technologies to participate in traditional civic activities (voting, engaging in public debate, protesting, paying taxes, etc.).

5. There are, of course, important strategic reasons that governments permit certain forms of protest during wartime. For example, the government can point to the protest as evidence of success (e.g., protest as an example of "freedoms we're fighting for") or claim that peaceful, legal forms of protest should be understood as the "extremist" wing of dissent (thus figuring more extreme forms of protest as outside an acceptable framework). In addition, one needs only to recall the Bush administration's "free speech zones" as a reminder of how variable this freedom can actually be.

6. Examples would include the elections of Anti-Corn League Association members John Bright and Richard Cobden in the early 1840s.

7. Laclau and Mouffe talk about this process as the annulment of the positivity of the object in order "to give a real existence to negativity as such" (128–29).

8. This seems especially true when institutions fail to effectively regulate the use of certain technologies.

9. From *The Jargon File*: "The lowest form of cracker; script kiddies do mischief with scripts and rootkits written by others, often without understanding the exploit they are using. Used of people with limited technical expertise...the adverse impact of such actions is usually minimal."

10. From *The Jargon File*: "Warez d00dz get illegal copies of copyrighted software. If it has copy protection on it, they break the protection so the software can be copied. Then they distribute it around the world via several gateways."

11. "This highly classified $6 billion program aims to secure the dot-gov and dot-mil domains by instituting basic security measures for federal agencies. These include installing improved monitor programs—known as "Einstein"—to detect intrusions on federal computers, for example, and sharing attack information across federal departments" ("U.S. Infrastructure").

12. "USCYBERCOM plans, coordinates, integrates, synchronizes, and conducts activities to: direct the operations and defense of specified Department of Defense information networks and; prepare to, and when directed, conduct full-spectrum military cyberspace operations in order to enable actions in all domains, ensure US/Allied freedom of action in cyberspace and deny the same to our adversaries."—U.S. Department of Defense, U.S. Cyber Command Fact Sheet, 25 May 2010

13. An early response from the hacktivist community, however, does little to suggest that a new ethics might be hacked out of this opportunity. In the days following the attack on Palin's account, hacktivists took exception to Bill O'Reilly's comments about the sharing of information. Shortly after his response, they posted one of their own—screenshots of information about the most recent subscribers to his premium Web service—information that they had obtained by hacking FoxNews' Web site.

14. Their status as "hackers" or as "hacktivists" is contested by many outside observers, including other hackers and hacktivists.

15. A Google News search reveals more than 1,900 news stories containing the words "Assange" and "Terrorist" from late 2010 to early 2011 ("Assange and Terrorist").

16. We refer here, in part, to ARPANET, the U.S. military program that was influential in the creation of the Internet. The final ARPANET report, detailing the project, can be accessed at www.archive.org.

17 This is a crude definition of the hacker ethic, at best. For a better brief description, see Internet publication *The Jargon File*. For a detailed survey of the origins of hacking and the hacker ethic, see Steven Levy's book *Hackers*.

18. Our discussion of obfuscation here could be related to Quintilian's notion of *skotison*, or a darkening and obscuring of speech. Lanham writes: "A number of rhetorical figures—all the figures of brevity, ellipsis, and implication, for example, really draw from the same well, though perhaps with a more peaceable intention. Often the rhetorical figures act as self-interference rituals, little self-and-other mystifications we perform just for the formal pleasure of it" (142).

8

Conclusion

Our contemporary moment is marked by dizzying flows of information, a discursive cacophony that is increasingly multi-mediated, transportable, and pervasive. Our political communication is shaped, in part, by the many capacities of new media technology—political blogs, mobile phone applications, viral videos, hyperlinking, and other forms of persistent and archived public discourse that continue to alter the political landscape. In this book we have suggested some specific modes through which we can analyze this phenomenon, its impact on the public and private spheres and the audiences therein, and its significance as rhetoric. In closing, we offer a brief summary of the ideas presented in the preceding chapters as well as some thoughts about future research into the rhetoric of new media.

As noted in our discussion of Michael Warner's work in Chapter 1, online discussion of political issues influences public awareness of and reactions to political developments. If we think of a public as a social space created by reflexive circulation of discourse, it is important to consider the role of circulating online texts in creating political constituencies and mobilizing user awareness and response. Constituencies and interest groups respond quickly to events such as the televised and YouTube presidential debate between Barack Obama and John McCain in October 2008, which featured questions posed by audience members who were present as well as by an online audience viewing the debate remotely. As Smith and

McDonald have observed, "Participatory forms of media production and circulation have . . . contested (our) understandings of citizenry as merely passive receivers of media content and political rhetoric. Rather, citizens are taking an active role in political and public participation" and they note that "scholars of media and political communication must explore new ways of theorizing the argumentation and deliberation processes in an age of digital media" (Smith & McDonald 123). We concur, and believe that continued study of these kinds of mergers between old and new media will be important to understanding the relationship between traditional and emerging models of political communication.

As was stated in the first edition, it is advisable for rhetorical critics and analysts to consider systematically the changes in persuasive processes made possible by the development of new forms of media use. For example, the presence of political news blogs and their increasing efforts to generate interactive public discussion by readers and contributors has expanded the reach and potentiality of public sphere participation and discussion. We have tried to illustrate this idea at several points in this book through rhetorical analysis. For example, as described in Chapter 2, the controversy surrounding the payment of AIG bonuses to corporate employees was widely treated online by means of statements and contributions by financial observers and consultants, and it was enhanced as well by input from bloggers well schooled in the financial sector who seem to have played a strong role in the adjustments made in proposed punitive legislation against the bonus payouts in Congress. In the long term, the Obama administration developed and implemented a plan that was more widely acceptable to various constituencies. In this case, well-informed online advocacy was pertinent to the situation and potentially useful to decision makers seeking a solution to the issue at hand.

While tracking how these developments affect political deliberation and capture public attention, we have also considered the role of online political parody in shaping the public's views of and interest in politics. As Robert Hariman has noted:

> Parody does not stop with ambiguity. What begins as a binary reversal . . . ultimately can put the binary under erasure.[1] The full significance of the parodic function is evident when placing a parody and its target discourse side by side. . . . Once set beside itself, not only that discourse but the entire system is destabilized
>
> Now there are two possible responses to any discourse: that which it intends and the laughter of those who see it through the lens of its parodic double. (Hariman, 254).

Our descriptions of online responses, contestation, debate, and resolution during the course of the election season have emphasized theIinternet's capacity as a forum for political decision-making as enabled by online news, user involvement, and mutual influence. Parody functions similarly to media framing,[2] a media strategy in which frames set a context that enables audiences to interpret media content in a certain way so as to shape interpretations of the material to which they are exposed (Scheufele, 106).

Examples of parodies intended to cast their subject in a negative light were presented in Chapter 5 with the *Huffington Post*'s parodies of Sarah Palin by Sara Benincasa, Liz Cackowski, Mercy Malick, Gina Gershon, and Tina Fey, and the *Jib Jab* parody of consumer outlet Walmart in the same chapter. In the Palin parody, the portrayal of the candidate's persona was designed to diminish her stature from political candidate to conventional housewife and mother, thus shifting audience perceptions of her experience and political leanings. The *JibJab* parody functioned to shift public awareness of Walmart's activities as a merchandiser of affordable goods and convenient shopping to one of an entity which exploited its employees and sent jobs overseas.

The structure of the Internet is such that use of parody as commentary on political events and developments can be quite effective. It is persuasive in that parody provides a context in which readers, viewers, and listeners are encouraged to consider political events, candidates, and positions in a situation that enables audience awareness of aspects of political activity of which they might otherwise be unaware. The chapter illustrated the importance of both internal and external intertextuality in online parodies of and in commentary about political developments and decision making. Furthermore, the opportunities that site creators and their audiences now enjoy to implement clever uses of intertextuality, suggestive allusion, and representation enable readers and respondents to interpret and act upon political issues, thus becoming more sophisticated and informed about the political stakes that affect their lives.

Our emphases on interactivity in Chapter 3 and intertextuality in Chapter 5 reveal the capacities of bloggers and their online respondents to develop shared understandings about major political events, and the results of such collaborations add value to their readers' understanding of the events they discuss. The roles played by interactivity during the midterm election cycle were apparent in the innovations introduced on the Democratic National Committee's Web site, "Organizing for America." The site included a number of features designed to attract user interest, participation, and involvement. They included sign-ups, maps identifying which candidates were campaigning in the various states, and appeals to users to take action in support of repealing "Don't Ask Don't Tell." Every effort was made to enhance user involvement, and there was ongoing discussion of issues in the site's interactive blog.

Chapter 3 also included extensive discussion and analysis of a posted user-based blog debate about commentary aired on the *Parker Spitzer Show* concerning

President Obama's tendency to yield too readily to compromises with the GOP on various issues, including tax cuts for the wealthy. This example illustrated the importance of interactivity in online public deliberation and discussion of political issues and events. In Chapter 4, our analysis of viral video, which highlighted how memes circulate, further extended this discussion of interactivity by highlighting the ways in which Lady Gaga's YouTube message to the Congress was taken up in various ways.

These texts also continue to operate in new contexts. Without question, one of the most significant developments in popular uses of new media over the past five years has been the exponential growth of social media. Today, social media encompass a wide range of technologies, including but not limited to social and professional networking websites, mobile check-in applications, and personal news feeds. Though the impact of these technologies on political processes and discourses has been touched on extensively in this book, the reach of popular sites like Facebook or Twitter extends well beyond the political realm.

For example, in chapter 2 we discussed that while in past campaigns we saw candidate efforts to mobilize supporters into offline groups as a way of solidifying their support base, in 2010 this strategy appeared to become secondary as campaign strategists turned more toward social networking and mobile communication as a means to reach out to potential supporters. Insofar as they were successful, observers had the opportunities to realize how various constituencies could speak their minds and discuss the means by which their priorities and values could be acknowledged and appropriated. Clever uses of intertextuality, puzzle solving, and suggestive allusion work on the Web and across social media all were used politically to imply positions and points of view that encouraged users to supply content and piece together conclusions from the clues supplied in the text. These texts function like enthymemes, since users work through the texts by supplying the missing inferences as they go.

Furthermore, we argued in Chapter 6 that both political and non-political uses of social media might be productively analyzed using several traditional rhetorical concepts such as Burkean identification, constitutive rhetoric, or other approaches such as narrative analysis. We have also discussed how a constitutive view of social networking technologies may help us understand something about how the concept of identity itself has shifted in the contemporary context. That is, while users of social networking sites often construct their own individual identities from bottom-up, the public's widespread use of social media has shifted the understanding of how identity itself might be constituted in the first place.

Concurrent with the growth of social media has been a greater public awareness of anti-institutional politics, those rhetorics of protest and radical action that are likewise constrained and enabled by a context of digitality and by a climate of both legitimate concern and misplaced paranoia about cyber-security. We argued in Chapter 7 that studying hacktivism provides the critic with examples for what it might mean to think about concepts like space and time, obfuscation, presence and absence, content and form, or publicity within new media contexts. Specifically, we suggested that these concepts can help us rethink how rhetorical process function within digital contexts.

Ultimately, throughout this project we have demonstrated that rhetorical theory offers a rich set of critical, analytical tools that can be productively used to make sense of the impact of new media in a variety of political discourses. We cannot, of course, predict how technology will change in the short or long term, which of the examples we've discussed in the preceding chapters will continue to be relevant into the future, or how transforming political climates will prompt new kinds of discourse. What we can be certain about is that the history and theory of rhetoric can continue to be applied to whatever might appear on the horizon.

Notes

1. A concept is said to be "under erasure" when it is put in question or under critique. This signifying practice, employed by Martin Heidegger and, after him, by Jacques Derrida and other deconstructive critics, is described by Gayatri Spivak as "to write a word, cross it out, and then print both word and deletion. (Since the word is inaccurate, it is crossed out. Since it is necessary, it remains legible.)" (Garber)

2. As Robert Entman has noted, Media frames are customarily viewed as aspects of journalistic discourse in that their context is defined as follows: "to frame is to select some aspects of a perceived reality and make them more salient in a communicating context, in such a way as to promote a particular problem definition, causal interpretation....Or moral evaluation " (52)

Works Cited

"50 Cent, Gilbert Gottfried Mock Japan's Earthquake Victims on Twitter." *FoxNews.com*, 14 Mar. 2011. Web. 29 May 2011.

Adams, John C. "Rhetoric's Teaching and Multi-modal Learning." *Academic Exchange Quarterly* (Fall 2006). Web. 24 Apr. 2011.

Aguiluz, Erine. "Jobless Americans still Struggling after Expiration of Unemployment Benefits." *Philadelphia Employment Law News*, 15 Dec. 2010. Web. 7 Jan 2011.

"Allegory." *Cambridge Dictionaries Online*, n.d. Web. 24 Apr. 2011.

Allen, Graham. *Intertextuality*. London: Routledge, 2000. Print.

Anderson, Lynn. "Facebook for Charity?" *Surviving in the Social Media Jungle*, 1 May 2011. Web. 29 May 2011.

Apple Computing. Apple Macintosh Computer Advertisement, n.d. .Web. 24 Apr. 2011.

"Approaches to Cyber Intrusion Response [Electronic Resource]: Report to the President's Commission on Critical Infrastructure Protection." President's Commission on Critical Infrastructure Protection. Washington, DC, 1997.

Armitage, John. "Beyond Postmodernism? Paul Virilio's Hypermodern Cultural Theory." *CTheory.net*. 15 Nov 2000. Web. 12 May 2011.

Asen, Robert. "Seeking the 'Counter' in Counterpublics." *Communication Theory* 10.4 (2000): 424–47. Print.

"Assange and Terrorist." Google News Search. Web. 29 May 2011.

Bacon, Perry Jr. "Obama Defends White House Deal with GOP on Tax Cuts." *Washington Post*, 7 Dec. 2010. Web. 11 Jan. 2011.

Bakhtin, Mikhail M. *The Dialogic Imagination: Four Essays*. Trans. Caryl Emerson and Michael Holquist. Austin: University of Texas Press, 1981. Print.

Bancroft, Collette. "Political Ads Go Pop." *St. Petersburg Times*, 26 December 2003, 1E. Print.

Barbierri, Cody. "Foursquare: 5 Million Users, 25,000 New Ones a Day." *VentureBeat*, 8 Dec. 2010. Web. 9 Jan. 2011.

Barthes, Roland. *Image Music Text*. Trans. Stephen Heath. New York: Noonday Press, 1977. Print.

Baudrillard, Jean. *Simulacra and Simulation*. Ann Arbor: University of Michigan, 1994. Print.

Bianco, Jamie Skye. "Social Networking and Cloud Computing: Precarious Affordances for the "Prosumer" *Women's Studies Quarterly 37: 1 & 2* (2009): 303–312. Print

Baumann, Nick, and David Corn. "Is Lady Gaga a Better Politician Than Barack Obama?" *Mother Jones*, 21 Sept. 2010. Web. 31 Jan. 2011.

Baym, Nancy K. *Personal Connections in the Digital Age*. Cambridge: Polity, 2010. Print.

Begley, Bill. "Palin E-mail Hacker a Former KISD Student." *Kdhnews.com*, 3 Oct. 2008. Web. 29 May 2011.

Belzer, Richard B. "The AIG Bonuses, Part 2: The House Tax Bill." *Neutral Source*, 23 March 2009. Blog. 30 July 2010.

———. "The AIG Bonuses, Part 6: The House Considers a New Bill." *Neutral Source*, 1 Apr. 2009: Blog. 30 July 2010.

Benoit, William L., and Susan L. Brinson. "Queen Elizabeth's Image Repair Discourse: Insensitive Royal or Compassionate Queen?" *Public Relations Review* 25.2 (1999): 145–57. Print.

Bertelsen, Dale A. "Media Form and Government: Democracy as an Archetypal Image in the Electronic Age." *Communication Quarterly*, 40(4) (1992): 325–37. Print.

Bianco, Jamie Skye. "Social Networking and Cloud Computing: Precarious Affordances for the 'Prosumer'" *Women's Studies Quarterly*, 37:1 & 2 (Spring/Summer 2009). Print

Biesecker, Barbara A. "Rethinking the Rhetorical Situation from Within the Thematic of Differance." *Philosophy and Rhetoric* 22.2 (1989): 110–30. Print.

Bradley, Tahman, and Stephanie Smith. "Obama Needs 12 Stitches After Getting Whacked in the Lip." *ABC News.com*, 5 Aug. 2010. Web. 29 Apr. 2011.

Brant-Zawadzki, Alex. "A Time for Tea: A Tea Party Time Line." *Huffington Post*, 15 Apr. 2010. Web. 1 Oct. 2010.

"Brenda's Message to the Senate." *YouTube*, 17 Sept. 2010. Web. 31 Jan. 2011.

Brinson, Susan L., and William L. Benoit. "The Tarnished Star." *Management Communication Quarterly* 12.4 (1999): 483–511. Print.

Brock, Jack. L. Computer Security Microform: Hackers Penetrate DOD Computer Systems: Statement of Jack L. Brock, Jr., Director, Government Information and Financial Management, Information Management and Technology Division, before the Subcommittee on Government Information and Regulation, Committee on Governmental Affairs, United States Senate. Washington, D.C.: U.S. General Accounting Office, 1991. Print.

Broersma, Matthew. "Activists Unveil Stealth Browser." *ZDNet UK*, 22 Sept. 2006. Web. 29 July 2011.

Browning, Bill. "IN07: Campaign Manager Tweets Anti-Gay Slurs." *Bilerico Project*, 13 Sept. 2010. Web. 09 January 2011.

Brustein, Joshua. "Advertise on NYTimes.com Nation's Political Pulse, Taken Using Net Chatter." *New York Times*, sec. 31: B4. Oct. 2010. Web. 09 January 2011.

Bucy, Eric P. "Interactivity in Society: Locating an Elusive Concept." *Information Society* 20 (2004): 373–83. Print.

Burke, Kenneth. *A Rhetoric of Motives*. Berkeley: University of California Press, 1950. Print.

———. *The Philosophy of Literary Form*. 3rd ed. Berkeley: University of California Press, 1973. Print.

Burnett, Robert, and P. David Marshall. *Web Theory: An Introduction*. London: Routledge, 2003. Print.

Carlson, Nicholas. "'Despicable, Slimy, Scummy Websites' Take Revenge on Bill O'Reilly." *Gawker*, 24 Sept. 2008. Web. 29 May 2011.

Carr, Austin. "Sorry, Facebook Fans, Likes Not Correlated to Mid-Term Election Success: Study." *FastCompany.com*, 15 Nov. 2010. Web. 29 May 2011.

Castells, Manuel. *Communication Power*. Oxford: Oxford University Press, 2009. Print.

CBS Interactive. "Michelle Obama Can't Escape Criticism on Vacation." 5 Aug. 2010. Web. 29 Apr. 2011.

CBS News. "'Cyber-squatting' Midterm Elections—CBS News Video." 22 Sept. 2010. Web. 9 Jan. 2011.

———. "Good Reviews of Obama Speech." 21 Mar. 2008. Web. 7 Sept. 2010.

———. "Poll: Most Say 'Ground Zero Mosque' Is Inappropriate." 25 Aug. 2010. Web. 8 May 2011.

Chadwick, Andrew. *Internet Politics*. New York: Oxford UP, 2006. Print.

Charland, Maurice. "Constitutive Rhetoric: The Case of the *Peuple Quebecois*." *Quarterly Journal of Speech* 73.2 (1987): 133–50. Print.

Chayko, Mary. *Portable Communities: The Social Dynamics of Online and Mobile Connectedness*. Albany: SUNY Press, 2008. Print.

"Chinese Hackers Invade 2 Official U.S. Web Sites." *New York Times*, 29 Apr. 2001, sec. 1:10. Print.

Cho, David, and Binyamin Appelbaum. "Bank Repayments May Exceed Estimate." *Washington Post*, 6 June 2009, Washington Post Co., 30 July 2010. Print.

Christ, Paul. "Foursquare Geo-Social Network Captures Marketer's Attention." KnowThis.com: Marketing Tutorials, News, How-to and More, 29 Apr. 2010. Web. 9 Jan. 2011.

"Christine O'Donnell: I'm Not a Witch." *YouTube*, 4 Oct. 2010. Web. 9 Jan. 2011.

"Christine O'Donnell: I'm You." *YouTube*, 4 Oct. 2010. Web. 9 Jan. 2011.

"Christine O'Donnell Practiced Witchcraft (BEST QUALITY)." *YouTube*, 17 Sept. 2010. Web. 9 Jan. 2011.

Cicero. "Treatise on Rhetorical Invention." c84. Trans. C. D. Yonge. *The Orations of Marcus Tullius Cicero*. London: George Bell & Sons, 1888. Print.

"CIA Hacked." *2600: Hacker Quarterly*, n.d. Web. 30 May 2011.

"CNN—Hacked CIA Web Site Due Back Soon—Sept. 23, 1996." *CNN.com*, 23 Sept. 2006. Web. 30 May 2011.

Coleman, Kevin. "Al Qaeda's Top Cyber Terrorist." *Defense Tech*, 26 Jan. 2008. Web. 29 May 2011.

Condon, Stephanie. "Sarah Palin Compares Hacking Case to Watergate—Political Hotsheet—CBS News." *CBS News*, 30 Apr. 2010. Web. 29 May 2011.

"Create a Social Networking Site with Ning, the Best Social Site Platform." *Ning*. Web. 9 Jan. 2011.

Darcy, Jeff. "Editorial Cartoon: Bush Signs Memo for Obama." *Plain Dealer*, 12 Nov. 2010. Web. 12 Nov. 2010.

"David Kernell Got 1 Year for Hacking Sarah Palin's Email." *Cyberbullying Report: Anti-Bullying and Internet Safety Services*, n.d. Web. 29 May 2011.

Dawkins, Richard. *The Selfish Gene*. Oxford: Oxford UP, 1989. Print.

Dean, Jodi. "Community." *Unspun: Key Concepts for Understanding the World Wide Web*. Ed. Thomas Swiss. New York: New York University Press, 2000. 4–16. Print.

Deem, Melissa. "Stranger Sociability, Public Hope, and the Limits of Political Transformation." *Quarterly Journal of Speech* 88.4 (2002): 444–54. Print.

DeLuca, Kevin M. *Image Politics: The New Rhetoric of Environmental Activism*. New York: Guilford, 1999. Print.

Democratic National Committee. *Organizing for America*. Blog. 7 Dec. 2010. Web. 4 Feb. 2011.

Denning, Dorothy. "Cyberwarriors: Activists and Terrorists Turn to Cyberspace." *Harvard International Review* 23.2 (2001): 70–75. Print.

Denning, D. (2000). "Hacktivism: An Emerging Threat to Diplomacy." *Foreign Service Journal*. Sept. 2000. Web. 18 Apr. 2011.

DieTryin.com. Remarks by Governor BushLite, June 12, 1999. Web.

Dionne, E. J. "Wealthy and Powerful Interests Are Out to Buy Elections This Year." *Pittsburgh Post Gazette.com*, 12 Oct. 2010. Web. 18 Apr. 2011.

"Domino's Charity Cycle." *Welcome to Facebook*, n.d. Web. 29 May 2011.

"Domino's Finds Social Media Marketing Is Secret Sauce to Profits in UK News [Brafton]." *Brafton News Content Marketing*, 13 July 2010. Web. 29 May 2011.

"Don't Ask Don't Tell Repealed DADT, KKK Response, Lady GaGa, News, Video." *YouTube*, 18 Sept. 2010. Web. 31 Jan. 2011.

"DoubleClick Ad Planner by Google—Site Profile of Myspace.com." n.d. *Google*. Web. 29 May 2011.

Dreyfus, Hubert. *On the Internet*. London: Routledge, 2001. Print.

Eastman, John C., and Marisa Maleck. "AIG Bonus Payments." New Federal Initiatives Project, 13 Apr. 2009. 7 Sept. 2010.

"Ed Martin Is Hackman." *Ed Martin Is Hackman*, n.d. Web. 9 Jan. 2011.

Endres, Danielle, and Barbara Warnick. "Text-based Interactivity in Candidate Campaign Web Sites: A Case Study from the 2002 Elections." *Western Journal of Communication* 68.3 (2004): 322–42. Print.

Entman, Robert M. "Framing: Toward Clarification of a Fractured Paradigm." *Journal of Communication* 43.4 (1993) 51-58. Print.

"Facebook's Privacy Policy." *Welcome to Facebook*, 22 Apr. 2010. Web. 5 Sept. 2010.

"FBI—Hearing on Cyber Terrorism." *FBI Homepage*, 24 Feb. 2004. Web. 29 May 2011.

Foot, Kirsten A., and Steven M. Schneider. *Web Campaigning*. Cambridge, MA: MIT Press, 2006. Print.

Foot, Kirsten A., Steven M. Schneider, and Michael Xenos. "Online Campaigning in the 2002 U.W. Elections." Working Paper version 2. (Earlier version presented at the Internet Research 3.0 Conference, Maastricht, the Netherlands, October 2002). Web. 24 Dec. 2005.

Foss, Sonja K. *Rhetorical Criticism: Exploration and Practice* (2nd ed.). Prospect, IL: Waveland Press, 1995. Print.

"Foursquare." *Foursquare*. 2010. Web. 1 Feb. 2011.

Fram, Alan. "Americans Dislike Democrats, Republicans Alike, Poll Finds." *AzCentral.com Associated Press*, 24 Sept. 2010. Web. 29 Jan 2011.

Fraser, Nancy, "Rethinking the Public Sphere: A Contribution to the Critique of Actually Existing Democracy." *Social Text* 25/26 (1990): 56–80. Print.

Froomkin, Michael. "How's Obama Doing, a Debate." *Discourse.net*. Blog. 20 Jan. 2010. Web. 29 Jan. 2011.

"Full List—Who Will Be TIME's 2010 Person of the Year?" *TIME.com*, 2010. Web. 1 Feb. 2011.

Gallup. Gallup Daily: Obama Job Approval, n.d. Web. 30 Jan. 2011.

Garber, Marjorie B. *Profiling Shakespeare.* New York: Routledge, 2008. Print

Gitelman, Lisa. *Always Already New: Media, History, and the Data of Culture.* Cambridge, MA: MIT Press, 2006. Print.

Gitelman, Lisa, and Geoffrey Pingree, eds. *New Media, 1740–1915.* Cambridge, MA: MIT Press, 2003. Print.

Gladwell, Malcom. "News Desk: Does Egypt Need Twitter?" *New Yorker*, 2 Feb. 2011. Web. 29 May 2011.

Good, Robin. "How Difficult Is It to Access Top Secret Information On US Military Computers?" *Professional Online Publishing: New Media Trends, Communication Skills, Online Marketing—Robin Good's MasterNewMedia*, 25 July 2005. Web. 29 May 2011.

Goodin, Dan. "Taking Aim at Cyberterrorism—CNET News." *CNET News*, 22 Oct. 1997. Web. 29 May 2011.

"Google Zeitgeist 2010." *Google*, 2010. Web. 1 Feb. 2011.

"Governor Sarah Palin's Yahoo Account Hacked! [UPDATE]." *Stop The Attacks.org*, 18 Sept. 2008. Web. 29 May 2011.

Green, Joshua. "'The Myth of Cyberterrorism' by Joshua Green." *Washington Monthly*, Nov. 2002. Web. 29 May 2011.

Gross, Alan G. "Presence as Argument in the Public Sphere." *Rhetoric Society Quarterly* 35.2 (2005): 5–21. Print.

Gurak, Laura. *The Rhetorical Dynamics of a Community Protest in Cyberspace: The Case of Lotus Marketplace.* Rochester, NY: Rensselaer Polytechnic Institute, 1994. Print.

H., E.H. "Report: Fair and Balanced Fox News Aggressively Promotes 'Tea Party' Protests." *Media Matters*, 8 Apr. 2009. Web. 1 Oct. 2010.

Habermas, Jürgen. *The Structural Transformation of the Public Sphere: An Inquiry into a Category of Bourgeois Society.* Trans. Thomas Burger with the assistance of Frederick Lawrence. Cambridge: MIT Press, 1989. Published originally in German as *Strukturwandel der Offentlicheit* in 1962. Print.

"Hackers Threaten U.S. Military Security, Lawmaker Says." *AP State & Local Wire*, 7 Mar. 1999. Web.

"Hacking U.S. Government Computers from Overseas." *Internet Archive Wayback Machine.* Western Region Security Office. 18 Nov. 2001. Web. 29 May 2011.

Hall, Stuart. *Critical Dialogues in Cultural Studies.* London: Routledge, 1996. Print.

———. "On Postmodernism and Articulation." *Journal of Communication Inquiry* 10 (1986): 45. *Communication and Mass Media Complete.* Print. 7 July 2011.

———. "Race, Articulation, and Societies Structured in Dominance." Baker, Houston A., Manthia Diawara, and Ruth H. Lindeborg. *Black British Cultural Studies:Aa Reader.* Chicago: University of Chicago, 1996. Print.

Hamilton, Anita. "Where the Hell Is Matt? (2008)—The Top 10 Everything of 2008—TIME." *TIME.com*, 3 Nov. 2008. Web. 1 Feb. 2011.

"Hamster on a Piano (Eating Popcorn)." *YouTube*, 25 Apr. 2010. Web. 31 Jan. 2011.

"Hamster on a Piano Ringtone." *Free Ringtone, Free Wallpaper, Free Games, Free Video for the Mobile Phone.* 15 Dec. 2008. Web. 31 Jan. 2011.

Hariman, Robert. "Political Parody and Public Culture." *Quarterly Journal of Speech* 94.3 (2008): 247–72. Print.

Hart, Roderick P. *Modern Rhetorical Criticism.* Boston: Allyn and Bacon, 1997. Print.

Hauser, Gerard A. *Vernacular Voices.* Columbia: University of South Carolina Press, 1999. Print.

Hebdige, Dick. *Subculture: The Meaning of Style.* London: Routledge, 1979. Print.

Hess, Aaron. "Resistance Up in Smoke: Analyzing the Limitations of Deliberation on YouTube." *Critical Studies in Media Communication* 26.5 (2009): 411–34. Print.

Hitchon, Jacqueline C., and Jerzy O. Jura. "Allegorically Speaking: Intertextuality of the Postmodern Culture and Its Impact on Print and Television Advertising." *Communication Studies* 48.2(1997): 142–58. *Communication and Mass Media Complete.* Web. 26 Apr. 2011.

Hirschkorn, Phil. "CNN.com—British National Indicted in Military Hacking Case." *CNN.com*, 12 Nov. 2002. Web. 29 May 2011.

"How Social Media Impacted the 2010 Midterm Elections—Press Release Distribution—PR NewsChannel." *PR NewsChannel*, 2 Nov. 2011. Web. 29 May 2011.

Huffington Post.com. "Happy 47th Birthday Sarah Palin! Here's 47 Seconds of Her Funniest Parodies." *HUFFPOST COMEDY*, n.d. Web Video. 28 Apr. 2011.

———. "Obama's Weekly Address Video: President Blasts Supreme Court over Citizens United Decision." 23 Jan. 2010. Web. 29 Jan. 2011.

———. "President Obama Defends Himself in Hilarious Musical Send Up." 14 Dec. 2010. Web. 24 Apr. 2011.

"Identity Squatting Can Cost Members of Congress Their Reputation." *CADNA—The Coalition Against Domain Name Abuse*, 15 Sept. 2010. Web. 9 Jan. 2011.

"I Voted." *Foursquare*, n.d. Web. 9 Jan. 2011.

"IMVU~Lady GaGa on Don't Ask Don't Tell." *YouTube*, 18 Sept. 2010. Web. 31 Jan. 2011.

Ingham, Tim. "PSN Suffers Black Wednesday—but Technology's Terrorists Won't Stop at Sony." *ComputerAndVideoGames.com*, 27 Apr. 2011. Web. 29 May 2011.

Institute for Politics, Democracy, and the Internet (IDPI). *Online Campaigning 2002.* Washington, DC: IDPI, 2002. Web. 30 Dec. 2002 from *Democracy Online.org.*

"Interpellation (philosophy)." *Wikipedia, the Free Encyclopedia.* 1 May 2011. Web. 30 May 2011.

Irwin, William. "Against Intertextuality." *Philosophy and Literature* 28.2 (2004): 227–42. *Project Muse.* Web. Accessed University of Pittsburgh. 2 Mar. 2011.

"ITunes—Everything You Need to Be Entertained." *Apple*, n.d. Web. 9 Jan. 2011.

"Jack Conway for Kentucky." *Welcome to Facebook*, n.d. Web. 29 May 2011.

Jenkins, Henry. *Textual Poachers: Television Fans & Participatory Culture.* New York: Routledge, 1992. Print.

JibJab Media. "Big Box Mart." n.d. 2005.Web. Animation. 29 Apr. 2011.

———. "So Long to Ya, 2010: The JibJab 2010 Year in Review!" Web. Video. n.d. 28 Apr. 2011.

———. "The Writing Process." Dec. 2010. Web. 28 Apr. 2011.

Johnson, Davi. "Mapping the Meme: A Geographical Approach to Materialist Rhetorical Criticism." *Communication and Critical/Cultural Studies* 4.1 (2007): 27–50. Print.

Johnson, Tom, and Dave Perlmutter. "'The Facebook Election: New Media and the 2008 Election Campaign' Special Symposium." *Mass Communication & Society* 12.3 (2009): 375–76. Print.

Jordan, John W. "(Ad)Dressing the Body in Online Shopping Sites." *Critical Studies in Media Communication* 20.3 (2003): 248–68. Print.

Jordan, Tim. *Activism!: Direct Action, Hacktivism, and the Future of Society.* London: Reaktion Books, 2002. Print.

Jordan, Tim, and Paul A. Taylor. *Hacktivism and Cyberwars: Rebels with a Cause?* London: Routledge, 2004. Print.

Joy, Kevin. "Job Anger Common, but Airline Steward Snapped." *Columbus Dispatch.com*, 11 Aug. 2011. Web. 29 Apr. 2011.

Kahn, Richard, and Douglas Kellner. "Internet Subcultures and Oppositional Politics." *The Post-Subcultures Reader.* Eds. David Muggleton and Rupert Weinzierl. Oxford: Berg Publishers, 2004. Print.

Kaplan, Nancy. "Literacy beyond Books: Reading When All the World's a Web." *The World Wide Web and Contemporary Cultural Theory.* Eds. Andrew Herman and Thomas Swiss. New York: Routledge, 2000. 207–34.

"Kato Kaelin Keyboard Cat." Online Home of Tosh.0's Funny Viral Videos Hosted by Daniel Tosh, Comedy Central. Comedy Central, 28 May 2009. Web. 31 Jan. 2011.

Katz, Celeste. "Lady Gaga Goes to Bat for Ending 'Don't Ask, Don't Tell' by Calling Sens. Schumer, Gillibrand." *NY Daily News*, 18 Sept. 2010. Web. 31 Jan. 2011.

Kennedy, George. A., Ed. and Trans. *Aristotle on Rhetoric.* New York: Oxford University Press, 1991. Print.

Kephart III, John M., and Steven F. Rafferty. "'Yes We Can': Rhizomic Rhetorical Agency in Hyper-modern Campaign Ecologies." *Argumentation and Advocacy* 46. Summer (2009): 6–20. Print.

Kiousis, Spiro. "Interactivity: A Concept Explication." *New Media & Society* 4.3 (2002): 355–83. Web. 4 Feb. 2011.

Kolawole, Emi. "Palin 'Favorites' Photo that Claims Obama Is a 'Taliban Muslim.'" *Blog Directory (washingtonpost.com)*, 5 Nov. 2010. Web. 9 Jan. 2011.

Kristeva, Julia. *Desire in Language.* New York: Columbia University Press, 1980. Print.

Kustritz, Anne. "Slashing the Romance Narrative." *Journal of American Culture* 26.3 (2003): 371–85. Print.

Laclau, Ernesto, and Chantal Mouffe. *Hegemony and Socialist Strategy: Towards a Radical Democratic Politics.* 2nd ed. London: Verso, 2001. Print.

"Lady Gaga—Bad Romance." *YouTube*, 23 Nov. 2010. Web. 1 Feb. 2011.

"Lady Gaga—DADT." *YouTube*, 20 Sept. 2010. Web. 31 Jan. 2011.

Lanham, Richard A. *A Handlist of Rhetorical Terms.* Berkeley: University of California, 1991. Print.

Lawrence, Chris. "Pentagon Not GaGa for Lady Gaga—CNN Political Ticker—CNN.com Blogs." *CNN Political Ticker—CNN.com Blogs*, 20 Sept. 2010. Web. 31 Jan. 2011.

"LBJ Daisy Ad." *YouTube*, 26 Oct. 2006. Web. 9 Jan. 2011.

Lemke, Jay L. "Travels in Hypermodality." *Visual Communication* 1.3 (2002): 299–325. Print.

Lenhart, Amanda, and Susannah Fox. "Bloggers: A Portrait of the Internet's New Story Tellers." Washington, DC: Pew Internet and American Life Project. 2006. Web. 4 Sept. 2010.

Levy, Steven. *Hackers: Heroes of the Computer Revolution.* NY: Penguin Books, 1994. Print.

Luo, Michael. "G.O.P. Allies Drive Ad Spending Disparity." *New York Times*, 13 Sept. 2010. Web. 18 Apr. 2011.

Maguire, Mariangela, and Laila Fara Mohtar. "Performance and the Celebration of a Subaltern Counterpublic." *Text & Performance Quarterly* 14.3 (1994): 238. Print.

Malloy, Daniel. "2 Pittsburgh TV Stations Using Anti-Sestak Ads Again." *Pittsburgh Post-Gazette*, 16 July 2010. Web. 7 Sept. 2010.

Manovich, Lev. *The Language of New Media*. Cambridge, MA; London: MIT Press, 2001. Print.

Marikar, Sheila. "John Mayer Apologizes on Twitter: Sorry I Used 'N-Word.'" *ABCNews.com*, 11 Feb. 2011. Web. 29 May 2011.

Marshall, Garry. "Internet and Memetics." *Welcome to Principia Cybernetica Web*, 1998. Web. 1 Feb. 2011.

McCarthy, Caroline. "Nielsen: Twitter's Growing Really, Really, Really, Really Fast." *Technology News—CNET News*, 19 Mar. 2009. Web. 9 Jan. 2011.

McDevitt, Caitlin. "Domino's Learns Twitter, Facebook Lessons—Business—The Big Money—Msnbc.com." *Msnbc.com*, 29 Jan. 2010. Web. 29 May 2011.

McDonnell, Brandy. "Blake Shelton Apologizes for Offending Gays with Twitter Lyric Rewrite." *BAM'S Blog*, 5 May 2011. Web. 29 May 2011.

McMillan, Sally J. "Exploring Models of Interactivity from Multiple Research Traditions: Users, Documents, and Systems." *The Handbook of New Media*. Eds. L. Lievrouw and S. Livingstone. Thousand Oaks, CA: Sage, 2002. 163–82. Print.

"Meet the Press." *Msnbc Video: McConnell: Assange Is a 'High-Tech Terrorist.'* NBC. *Msnbc.com*, 5 Dec. 2010. Web. 29 May 2011.

Melucci, Alberto. "A Strange Kind of Newness: What's 'New' In New Social Movements?" *New Social Movements: From Ideology to Identity*. Eds. Hank Johnston, Enrique Larana and Joseph R. Gusfield. Philadelphia, PA: Temple University Press, 1994. 101-32. Print

"Members—Tea Party Nation." *Tea Party Nation*. Web. 9 Jan. 2011.

"Meme—WhatPort80." Main Page—WhatPort80, 20 Aug. 2010. Web. 1 Feb. 2011.

"Mendenhall's Tweets Stir up Controversy CBS Pittsburgh." *CBS Pittsburgh*, 3 May 2011. Web. 29 May 2011.

"A Message from Lady Gaga to the Senate Sept 16 2010." *YouTube*, 19 Sept. 2010. Web. 31 Jan. 2011.

"Military 'Hacker' Freed on Bail." *BBC News*, 8 June 2005. Web. 29 May 2011.

Montgomery, Justin. "Domino's Foursquare Rewards Promotion Helped Boost Revenue by 29%." *Mobile Marketing Watch*, 16 July 2010. Web. 29 May 2011.

"More Domino's." *Domino's*, n.d. Web. 29 May 2011.

Morozov, Evgeny. "Facebook and Twitter Are Just Places Revolutionaries Go." *Guardian*, 7 Mar. 2011. Web. 29 May 2011.

Muntean, Nick, and Anne H. Petersen. "Celebrity Twitter: Strategies of Intrusion and Disclosure in the Age of Technoculture." *M/C Journal* 12.5 (2009). Web. 29 May 2011.

Natharius, David. "The More We Know, the More We See: The Role of Visuality in Media Literacy." *American Behavioral Scientist* 48.2 (2004): 238–47. Print.

New Federal Initiatives Project. "AIG Bonus Payments." *The Federalist Society for Law and Public Policy Studies*, 13 April, 2009: The Federalist Society. Web 18 July 2010.

Newhagen, John E. "Interactivity, Dynamic Symbol Processing, and the Emergence of Content in Human Communication." *Information Society* 20 (2004): 395–400. Print.

Newman, Nathan. *TPM (Talking Points Memo)*, Aug. 2010. Web. 30 Jan 2011.

New York Times: Business Day. "Wal-Mart Stores Inc." 30 Mar. 2011. Web. 29 Apr. 2011.

Nielsen, Rasmus K. "Twitter in the Midterms." *Rasmuskleisnielsen.net*, 15 Nov. 2010. Web. 9 Jan. 2011.

"Nom Nom Nom Nom Nom Nom Nom—Parry Gripp." *YouTube*, 27 Feb. 2009. Web. 31 Jan. 2011.

"Number of Twitter Users." *Twitter Facts*, 22 July 2007. Web. 18 May 2011.

Ong, Walter J. *Orality and Literacy: The Technologizing of the Word*. London and New York: Routledge, 1982. Print.

Ono, Kent A. "Counterpublics and the State." *Argumentation and Advocacy* 40.11 (2003): 61–65. Print.

Ono, Kent A., and John M. Sloop. "The Critique of Vernacular Discourse." *Communication Monographs* 62 (1995): 19–46. Print.

O'Toole, James. "2 Television Stations to Pull Ad Critical of Sestak." *Post-Gazette.com Pittsburgh Post-Gazette*, 15 July 2010. Web. 17 July 2010.

Ott, Brian, and Cameron Walter. "Intertextuality: Interpretive Practice and Textual Strategy." *Critical Studies in Media Communication* 17.4 (2000): 429–46. Print.

Papacharissi, Zizi. *A Networked Self: Identity, Community and Culture on Social Network Sites*. New York: Routledge, 2011. Print.

"Papa John's Pizza (papajohns) on Twitter." *Twitter*. Web. 29 May 2011.

"Parody." *Cambridge Dictionaries Online*. Cambridge University Press, n.d. Web. 28 Apr. 2011.

Parramore, Lynn. "Let's Go Gaga: Time to Ask and Tell." *Huffington Post*, 22 Sept. 2010. Web. 31 Jan. 2011.

Parry-Giles, Shawn J., and J. Michael Hogan. *The Handbook of Rhetoric and Public Address*. Chichester, West Sussex, UK: Wiley-Blackwell, 2010. Print.

Petty, R. E., and J. T. Cacioppo. *Communication and Persuasion: Central and Peripheral Routes to Attitude Change*. New York: Springer-Verlag, 1986. Print.

Pfister, Damien S. Introduction: Public Argument/Digital Media. Spec. issue of *Argumentation and Advocacy* 47.2 (Fall 2010): 63–66. Print.

"President Barack Obama 2009 Inauguration and Address." *YouTube*, 20 Jan. 2009. Web. 1 Feb. 2011.

PRI's The World. "Tech Podcast: Wikileaks, Hacktivism, and Four Views of the 'Net.'" 19 Mar. 2010. Web. 1 Oct. 2010.

Pugh, Tony. "Recession Sent Millions More into Poverty." *Pittsburgh Post-Gazette*, 17 Sept. 2010. Web. 29 Jan. 2011.

Puopolo, Sonia "Tita." "The Web and U. S. Senatorial Campaigns." *American Behavioral Scientist* 44.12 (2001): 2030–47.

R34Mendenhall. *Clarification*. 4 May 2011. Web. 29 May 2011.

"'The Rachel Maddow Show' for Thursday, March 19, 2009—MsnbcTv—Rachel Maddow Show—Msnbc.com." *Msnbc.com*, 20 Mar. 2009. Web. 31 Jan. 2011.

Rafaeli, Sheizaf. "Interactivity: From New Media to Communication." *Sage Annual Review of Communication Research*. Eds. R. P. Hawkins, J. M. Weimann, and S. Pingree. Beverly Hills, CA: Sage, 1988. 110–34. Web. 5 Mar. 2004.

"Rand Paul." *Welcome to Facebook*. n.d. Web. 29 May 2011.

Rasmussen Reports. "Generic Congressional Ballot. October Ballot Survey." 4 Oct. 2010. Web. 18 Apr. 2011.

Raymond, Eric S. "The Jargon File, Version 4.4.8." *Jargon File Resources*, 1 Oct. 2004. Web. 29 May 2011.

"Remarks by Governor BushLite." *DieTryin.com*, 12 Jun. 1999. Web. 7 Jul. 2000.

Rice, Jesse. *The Church of Facebook: How the Hyperconnected Are Redefining Community*. Colorado Springs, CO: David C. Cook, 2009. Print.

Ricoeur, Paul. "Narrative Time." *Critical Inquiry* 7.1 (1980): 169–90. Print.

Riely, Kaitlynn. "Suspect in India Put Angry Posts on Facebook." *Pittsburgh Post-Gazette*, 19 Aug. 2010. Web. 5 Sept. 2010.

Rodriguez, Ashlie. "How Much Should Candidates Court the Web?" *NationalJournal.com*, 7 Nov. 2010. Web. 29 May 2011.

"Sarah Palin Faces Her Cyber Terror Nemesis." *CTI: Cyber Terror Investigation*, 25 Apr. 2010. Web. 29 May 2011.

"Satire." *Oxford Dictionaries*. Oxford University Press, n.d. 2011. Web. 28 Apr. 2011.

Scheufele, Dietram A. "Framing as a Theory of Media Effects" *Journal of Communication*, Winter (1999): 103–122. Print.

Schlesinger, Jennifer. "Did Facebook and Twitter Predict the 2010 Midterm Election Results?— ABC News." *ABCNews.com*, 25 Nov. 2010. Web. 29 May 2011.

Schneier, Bruce. "Here Comes Everybody Review." *Schneier on Security*. Blog. Web. 25 Nov. 2008. 30 Oct. 2010.

Scholes, Robert. *Protocols of Reading*. New Haven, CT: Yale University Press, 1989. Print.

Schudson, Michael. "Was There Ever a Public Sphere? If So, When? Reflections on the American Case." *Habermas and the Public Sphere*. Ed. Craig Calhoun. Cambridge, MA: MIT Press, 1992. Print.

Scola, Nancy. "For a Second Year, House Republicans Compete to Win the Internet." *TechPresident*, 10 May 2011. Web. 29 May 2011.

———. "Judging Foursquare-dom's Election Day Performance." *TechPresident*, 3 Nov. 2010. Web. 9 Jan. 2011.

Scott, Robert E. "The High Price of 'Free' Trade." Economic Policy Institute: Research and Ideas for Shared Prosperity, 17 Nov. 2003. Web. 29 Apr. 2011.

Selfe, Cynthia L. "The Movement of Air, the Breath of Meaning: Aurality and Multimodal Composing." *College Composition and Communication* 60.4 (2009): 616–63. Print.

Sewell, Abby. "Pew Report: Cellphone Use Widespread in 2010 Midterm Elections." *Los Angeles Times*, 23 Dec. 2010. Web. 9 Jan. 2011.

Shepard, Ryan. "Toward a Theory of Simulated Atonement: A Case Study of President George W. Bush's Response to the Abu Ghraib Torture." *Communication Studies* 60.5 (2009): 460–75. Print.

Shiels, Maggie. "BBC News—Twitter Co-founder Jack Dorsey Rejoins Company." *BBC Homepage*, 28 Mar. 2011. Web. 18 May 2011.

Shirky, Clay. *Here Comes Everybody: The Power of Organizing Without Organizations*. New York: Penguin Press 2008. Print.

Shribman, David. "Taming the Tea Party." *Pittsburgh Post-Gazette.com*, 3 Oct. 2010. Web. 31 Jan. 2011.

Sloop, John M., and Kent A. Ono. "Out-Law Discourse: The Critical Politics of Material Judgement." *Philosophy and Rhetoric* 30 (1997): 50–69. Print.

"Slowloris." *Wikipedia, the Free Encyclopedia.* Web. 29 July 2011.

Smith, Aaron. "The Internet and Campaign 2010: How Americans Used the Internet in Campaign 2010.," 17 Mar. 2011. Web. 15 May 2011.

———. "The Internet and the 2010 Campaign." *Pew Research Center's Internet & American Life Project,* 14 Apr. 2011. Web. 29 May 2011.

———. "The Internet's Role in Campaign 2008." *Pew Internet and American Life Project,* 15 April 2009. Web. 7 Jan. 2011.

Smith, Christina M., and Kelly M. McDonald. "The Arizona 9/11 Memorial: A Case Study in Public Dissent and Argumentation through Blogs." Spec. issue of *Argumentation and Advocacy* 47.2 (Fall 2010): 123–39. Print.

"Social Media, Cellphone Video Fuel Arab Protests." *The Independent Newspaper,* 27 Feb. 2011. Web. 29 May 2011.

Soffer, Oren. "The Textual Pendulum." *Communication Theory* 15.3 (2005): 266–91. Print.

"Something for Nothing!—Domino's Facebook Fundraiser Extended!" *Welcome to Facebook,* 16 Apr. 2010. Web. 29 May 2011.

"Songify This—I'M NOT A WITCH—Sung by Christine O'Donnell." *YouTube,* 16 Oct. 2010. Web. 9 Jan. 2011.

"Sony PlayStation Users: How to Fight a Data Breach." *FoxBusiness.com,* 4 May 2011. Web. 29 May 2011.

Spangler, Grace. "Fundraising in the 2010 Midterm Elections." *Future Leaders in Philanthropy,* 2 Nov. 2010. Web. 9 Jan. 2011.

Spivak, Gayatri Chakravorty. "Can the Subaltern Speak?." *The Postcolonial Studies Reader.* Ed.Bill Ashcroft. NY: Routledge, 1995. pp.24–8. Print.

"Spoof." *Dictionary.com,* n.d. 2011. Web. 28 Apr. 2011.

"Statistics." *Welcome to Facebook,* n.d. Web. 29 May 2011.

Stein, Kevin A. "Jewish Antapologia in Response to Mel Gibson's Multiple Attempts at Absolution." *Relevant Rhetoric: A New Journal of Rhetorical Studies* 1.1 (2010): 1–14. Web. 29 May 2011.

Stein, Sarah R. "The '1984' Macintosh Ad: Cinematic Icons and Constitutive Rhetoric in the Launch of a New Machine." *Quarterly Journal of Speech* 88.2 (2002): 169–92. Print.

Stromer-Galley, Jennifer. "On-Line Interaction and Why Candidates Avoid it." *Journal of Communication* 50.4 (2000): 111–32. Print.

Stromer-Galley, Jennifer, and Kirsten A. Foot. "Citizen Perceptions of Online Interactivity and Implications for Political Campaign Communication." *Journal of Computer-Mediated Communication* 8.1 (2002).Print.

Tarrow, Sidney. *Power in Movement: Social Movements and Contentious Politics.* 2nd ed. Cambridge: Cambridge University Press, 1998. Print.

Tea Party Nation, n.d. Web. 29 May 2011.

Terrill, Robert E. "Unity and Duality in Barack Obama's 'A More Perfect Union.'" *Quarterly Journal of Speech* 95.4 (2009): 363–86. Print.

Theye, Kirsten. "Shoot, I'm Sorry: An Examination of Narrative Functions and Effectiveness within Dick Cheney's Hunting Accident Apologia." *Southern Communication Journal* 73.2 (2008): 160–77. Print.

"Timeline." *Welcome to Facebook.* Web. 18 May 2011.

Toulmin, Stephen E. *The Uses of Argument.* Cambridge: Cambridge University Press, 1958. Print.

Towner, Emil B. "A Patriotic Apologia: The Transcendence of the Dixie Chicks." *Rhetoric Review* 29.3 (2010): 293–309. Print.

Turkle, Sherry. *Life on the Screen: Identity in the Age of the Internet.* New York: Simon and Schuster, 1997. Print.

Twitter. n.d. Web. 9 Jan. 2011.

"Twitter Feed F-Word Gets Chrysler Employee Fired—FoxNews.com." *FoxNews.com*, 10 Mar. 2011. Web. 29 May 2011.

United States. Department of Defense. Cyber Command. *U.S. Cyber Command Fact Sheet*, 25 May 2010. Web. 29 May 2011.

Uniting and Strengthening America by Providing Appropriate Tools Required to Intercept and Obstruct Terrorism (USA Patriot Act) Act of 2001. 107th Congress. 1st. H.R. 3162. 24 Oct. 2001.

"U.S. Infrastructure Remains Vulnerable to Cyber Terrorism." *Business News & Financial News— The Wall Street Journal—Wsj.com*, 21 Feb. 2009. Web. 29 May 2011.

"U.S. Web Sites Hacked, Fixed." *Pittsburgh Post-Gazette.* 30 April, 2001: A6. Print.

Video Café; Heather's Blog. "Anthony Weiner Asks President Obama to Quit Punting on Third Down." 7 Dec. 2010. Web. 7 Jan. 2011.

"Viral Video Chart—Greyson Chance Singing Paparazzi." *Viral Video Chart—Powered by Unruly Media*, 28 Apr. 2010. Web. 31 Jan. 2011.

Virilio, Paul. *The Aesthetics of Disappearance.* 1st English ed. New York: Semiotext(e), 1991. Print.

———. *Desert Screen: War at the Speed of Light.* London and New York: Continuum, 2002. Print.

———. *The Lost Dimension.* New York: Semiotext(e), 1991. Print.

———. *Pure War.* Foreign Agents. New York: Semiotext(e), 1983. Print.

———. *Speed and Politics.* New York: Semiotext(e), 1986. Print.

———. *War and Cinema: The Logistics of Perception.* London and New York: Verso, 1989. Print.

Voight, Joan. "Papa John's Pizza Contest Pairs Social Media and R&D." *ClickZ*, 9 Aug. 2010. Web. 29 May 2011.

Warner, Michael. "Publics and Counterpublics (Abbreviated Version)." *Quarterly Journal of Speech* 88.4 (2002): 413–25. Print.

———. "Publics and Counterpublics." *Public Culture* 14.1 (2002a): 49–90. Print.

Warnick, Barbara. *Critical Literacy in a Digital Era: Technology, Rhetoric, and the Public Interest.* Mahwah, NJ: Lawrence Erlbaum Associates, 2002. Print.

———. "The Rational and the Reasonable in the AIG Bonus Controversy." *Argumentation and Advocacy* (Fall 2009): 98–109. Print.

Warnick, Barbara, Michael Xenos, Danielle Endres, and John Gastil. "Effects of Campaign-to-User and Text-Based Interactivity in Political Candidate Campaign Web Sites." *Journal of Computer-Mediated Communication* 10.3 (2005): article 5. Print.

Washington & Lee University. "W & L Law Professor Discusses Legal Issues in AIG Bonus Controversy." 20 Mar. 2008. Web. Audio file. 7 Sept. 2010.

Weiner, Jeff. "The LinkedIn Blog, Blog Archive 100 Million Members and Counting . . ." *The LinkedIn Blog*, 22 Mar. 2011. Web. 29 May 2011.

Welch, Kathleen E. *Electric Rhetoric: Classical Rhetoric, Oralism, and a New Literacy.* Digital Communication. Cambridge, MA: MIT Press, 1999. Print.

White, R. J. *Radicalism and Its Results, 1760–1837*. Pamphlet. Aids for Teachers.

WikiLeaks. "About Wikileaks." Web. 27 Oct. 2010.

Wikimedia Foundation. Blog. Modified 25 July 2010. Web. 29 July 2010.

Wikipedia Foundation. *The Pirates of Penzance*. n.d. Web. 24 Apr. 2011.

"Willie Horton 1988 Attack Ad." *YouTube*, 3 Nov. 2008. Web. 9 Jan. 2011.

Wittenburg, David. "Going out in Public: Visibility and Anonymity in Michael Warner's 'Publics and Counterpublics.'" *Quarterly Journal of Speech* 88.4 (2002): 426–33. Print.

Wittkower, D. E. *Facebook and Philosophy: What's on Your Mind?* Chicago: Open Court, 2010. Print.

Wolfe, Dylan. "The Video Rhizome: Taking Technology Seriously in 'The Meatrix.'" *Environmental Communication* 3.3 (2009): 317–34. Print.

Yasinskas, Pat. "Bush Saying Farewell to New Orleans?—NFC South Blog—ESPN." *ESPN: The Worldwide Leader in Sports*, 29 Apr. 2011. Web. 29 May 2011.

Zappen, James P. "Digital Rhetoric: Towards an Integrated Theory." *Technical Communication Quarterly* 14.3 (2005): 319–25. Print.

Zittrain, Jonathan. *The Future of the Internet and How to Stop It*. New Haven and London: Yale University Press, 2008. Print.

Index